24.70

COMPUTER
ANIMATION

EXPERT ADVICE ON
BREAKING INTO THE BUSINESS

COMPUTER ANIMATION

EXPERT ADVICE ON BREAKING INTO THE BUSINESS

by

Dale K. Myers

Oak Cliff Press
Milford, Michigan
1999

Publisher's Cataloging-in-Publication Data

Myers, Dale K.
    Computer animation: expert advice on breaking into the business / Dale K. Myers

    Includes index.
    ISBN: 0-9662709-6-7

    1. Computer animation - Handbooks, manuals, etc. I. Title

TR897.5.M99 1999   006.6/96—dc21   99-62471

Library of Congress Catalog Card Number: 99-62471

PRINTED IN THE UNITED STATES OF AMERICA

For more information or to order additional copies, write:

Oak Cliff Press
P.O. Box 608
Milford, MI, 48381-0608

www.oakcliffpress.com

Dedicated to future animators everywhere

Only passions, great passions, can elevate the soul to great things.

Denis Diderot, *Pensees Philosophiques* (1746)

Table of Contents

Introduction

The world of computer animation and visual effects is arguably today's hottest profession. Technology has pumped new life into the entertainment business, creating a cry for talented animators, artists and creative people of all kinds.

It is unlikely that the demand for computer savvy artists will subside anytime soon. If anything, the need for people to handle the incredible explosion of motion pictures, commercials, and television programs that rely on computer effects will only grow exponentially. Writers, producers and directors have discovered a new tool that allows them to tell stories in a way never before imagined. The genie is out of the bottle, and no one is looking for the cork.

Navigating the uncertain waters of this burgeoning industry can be dangerous, especially for those entering the field. Making decisions about schooling, software, demo reels, and job prospects can be overwhelming without inside information. Hence, the reason for this long overdue guide.

I've been involved in computer animation for more than ten years, and in that time have acquired a wealth of knowledge and experience about what it *really* takes to be successful in this exciting field. Over the past year, I've spoken with dozens of animation and visual effects experts who have verified and - in some cases - expanded on the advice presented in this volume. These combined experiences have been distilled into the street-smart guide you hold in your hand.

Trying to figure out how to break into the business can be an exercise in frustration. Maybe you've talked with friends and family. Maybe you have a friend in the business. Maybe you're like I was - a ton of desire and not a clue in the world.

Think of this book as your pocket mentor. You won't find any techniques or instructions on how to create animation in this work. What you will find is a gold mine of candid, practical advice that you can put to good use today - right now! If you take heed, I promise you'll avoid years of heartaches and mistakes that plagued those who blazed the trail before you.

So, unplug the phone, disconnect the doorbell, grab a yellow highlight marker, and settle down in a comfortable chair. The keys to your future are just ahead.

Chapter 1:
Getting Started

The most important thing you can do is to take *action*!

You've already taken the first step - and that's good. But it's not good enough. Having a desire to get into computer animation and making it happen are two different things.

Desire is only a foundation. You've got to learn to turn desire into *action*. I know you've got what it takes. The fact that you're reading this book means that you've already taken the first *action* step toward fulfilling your dream. And just like a toddler, you need only take another step, and still another. Soon, you'll be where you want to be.

I knew a guy who wanted to be an animator, but he never took *action* to make his dream come true. I was teaching animation classes at a local computer store. "Joe" was a guy in his early twenties. His animations were quite good - above the norm. I urged him to put together a demo reel. But, week after week "Joe" would show up without a reel in hand. One day after class, I heard him talking about wanting to work out in Los Angeles at one of the major animation studios. I cornered him, "Have you got a demo reel, together?" "No," he replied. "How are you going to get a job without a demo reel?" He didn't know. Now, who's to say whether that conversation lit a fire, but one thing's for sure - "Joe" finally put together a demo reel and landed a job at that very L.A. studio.

You'll never get anywhere by standing still. You've got to take *action*!

Some students I've known are holding out for just the right moment. Yet, every second they wait costs them precious time. The reason is simple. Life is like a train, and you're standing on the station platform. A lot of people are waiting for the train to stop, so they can get aboard comfortably and at their own pace. The reality is that the train will *never* stop. It simply roars passed the station platform and races into the future. Now, you have a choice. You can wait and hope the train slows down - *something that will never happen.* Or, you can jump on board as it goes by. The sooner you get on board, the farther ahead you'll be. And believe me, there are a lot of people *just like you* who are itching to get on board that train! So, go ahead. Make the leap. I'll guarantee the ride is a lot of fun!

Ready to take action? Okay. Here's the single most important phrase you need to burn into your brain:

You must prove your ability.

That's right. *Prove* your ability. Think about it. Do you really think television producers are going to risk a $250,000 dollar budget - not to mention their reputation - on your unproven skill level?

You'd be surprised at how many people think someone owes them a job simply because they have a desire to try something new. Forget about your degree, or your vast experience in a related field. If you want to work as a computer animator, you've got to *prove* you can do it! Sorry, but there's no getting around it.

How do you go about proving your ability? The traditional approach (and the one you'll be expected to follow) is to put together a demo reel - a short collection of animations that *demonstrate* your abilities. Now, before we get into the nuances of building a demo reel, you need to develop your animation skills.

You've got three routes you can go:

(1.) Get a professional animator to teach you the ropes.

This is the least likely route. If you live near a studio, give it a shot. It doesn't hurt to ask, and most animators are friendly people. (Really!) But you're likely to find that most animators are too busy to devote time to your budding career.

More than likely, you'll follow one of these two directions:

(2.) Attend a college or trade school specializing in   animation, or

(3.) Teach yourself

Both options have advantages and disadvantages that you'll want to weigh carefully. And remember, there are *no guarantees* regardless of the route you pursue. Neither option means you'll become an animator, it only means you have the *opportunity to learn* how to become one.

Colleges and Animation Schools

Universities and animation trade schools are fast becoming a favorite choice for eager animation wannabes. They're taught by skilled animators, allow you to interact and share ideas with other students, and the best ones have connections within the industry to encourage placement upon graduation. The downside of attending a trade school is that they require on campus attendance (which may be in another state), and you'll share machine time with other students - something you can't afford to do when you're developing skill levels. Cost is another major factor. On top of tuition, you'll need money to sleep, eat, and buy animation supplies.

Course focus

There are a wide range of choices when it comes to selecting a curriculum. Experts in the field tend to favor courses that develop skills specific to their particular area of focus. Here are some suggestions:

Film

"If you go to school, take classes in film and art composition," says P.J. Foley, Visual Effects Supervisor with Foundation Imaging. "And then supplement it with practical, hands-on experience on a home computer. Learn film technique, editing, camera work and then go home and apply that knowledge to computer animation. My only regret is that I did not take more film classes."

"I never had the opportunity to go to film school," confirms John Allardice, Visual Effects Supervisor at Foundation Imaging. "But if anything will serve you in this business, it's a film education. It is *not* a technical education. Computing science is never going to help you be a better animator. But still, I think the best thing you can do is to just sit in a room and watch movie after movie. There is nothing - apart from making movies - that will give a better feel for how they are done than just watching them. When you spot a nice shot ask yourself, "Why does it look great?" Break it down. Pause the video a second. Check out the shadows on everybody's faces and figure out where the light is coming from. How many lights do they have on that set? Which ones are soft? Which ones are hard? Are there any nice little background reflections that really add to the shot? I've heard a lot of people say, "Look at real life." No. *Don't* look at real life. Real life isn't what people want to see in an effects shot. They want to see *movie* life, not real life. And movie life looks *completely* different than real life. The lighting is different, the colors are different, and the saturation's different. We ran into a perfect example of this at Digital Domain. A couple of us were doing some tests for *Air Force One*; the whole battle with the MIGS at the end. We bid on that. We spent three or four days trying to make it look real. We'd added film grain and diffused the hell out of it - really mucking with the image to make it look as real as possible. When we checked it out in the screening room, the producer turned around and said, 'Yea, it looks great! It looks like you were standing next to the DP with a 16mm Bolex. But, we can't cut this into a feature.' You see, we actually went too far. We made it so gritty, so dirty, so *real* that it looked like something out of a documentary. It didn't look like it was something out of a movie. So we had to back off on it, and make it a little less real life to get that movie feel into it."

Film & art

"To stand out, you need to have a depth of knowledge," explains John Follmer, Vice President and Head of Production at Metrolight Studios. "Technical skills are just *one* of the things that we're looking for. But somebody that has a knowledge of filmmaking becomes a valuable commodity because invariably what we're doing is creating film - *not* computer animation. So, to have that knowledge of traditional film is helpful. To have an art background is also very helpful. In fact, you can't have too much background in art, film, and photography."

"When I started in school, I didn't really know what direction I wanted to go," says Metrolight Studios animator Jeremie Talbot. "I knew it was this field. So, I went for a general art background, taking a visual communications type of curriculum. Along the way, I learned a lot about the art of filmmaking - something I wouldn't have learned at an animation school. The thing I did miss was the principles of animation, which I had to get on my own through talking to people, showing my reel, and studying, *Disney Animation: The Illusion of Life*, by Frank Thomas and Ollie Johnston."

Traditional animation

"I think learning 2D animation is the best way to go," advises Blue Sky Studios animator Doug Dooley. "Because, in 3D the computer starts interpolating the motion between keys - it starts doing it for you - and then people stop concentrating on what's happening. Traditional animators are so good, because they really focus on the movement of every little thing - the hair, the arms, where the hand is going. With the computer, you put a key frame here, you put one there, and it starts to figure the inbetweens for you. People see it moving and they lose the critical eye. So, I think learning how to animate frame-by-frame, in two dimensions, is a tremendous help in developing a critical eye for motion."

Art and design

"I studied industrial design which gave me a basis for general design theory," says Digital Muse creative director, Bruce Branit. "I focused on color theory, things like that. I find that quite valuable. It's interesting, there are a lot of people in this business with film backgrounds and so they understand things in terms of what they were taught in film school. I think there is a lot for me to learn from them, and a lot for them to learn from me in terms of composition, and the things I learned in design."

"First and foremost I would say just get a basic understanding of art itself," urges Rhythm & Hues Studios character animator Lyndon Barrois. "You *have* to have that. The fundamentals of those skills are *essential*. Learning computer skills alone is not enough. You have to know what to put into the computer. The computer does *nothing*. I don't care what version of Photoshop or Illustrator you have. If you have no clue how to draw, or know nothing about color theory, or composition and design, everything you do on a computer is going to look bad. So, learn all of the skills *practically* first. Learn how to do it from all aspects and then *apply* it to the computer. A lot of people tend to believe that a computer makes animation easier and it doesn't. It makes it easier because you can do things faster. But, you can do a lot of fast animation that looks horrible if you don't have the skills. It's like having a tool and not knowing what to do with it. And you see that a lot."

Technology and art

"I think if you have a broad palette to draw from for inspiration and a passion to make a statement, you're more likely to bring a unique point of view," says Paul Diener, Director of Digital Production at Will Vinton Studios. "The computer skills are a necessary complement because there is such a wide range of tools, and it's important to stay current with technology to support your aesthetic. But, I also think that storytelling, writing and filmmaking skills are also complementary mediums."

"I would recommend a good foundation of basic drawing skills and photography," says Robert Lurye, Lighting Director at Rhythm & Hues. "Some computer programming would certainly help so that you understand the concepts behind computers. A lot of programs have a higher level graphical interface, but they're ultimately based on computer logic. So maybe a little programming, C-Shell, scripting, that kind of thing. The more you know about the tools, the stronger you'll be. You can develop aesthetic sensibilities using computer tools, but I think there is something to be said for a traditional approach."

"Most students don't recognize that the computer is just a tool," says animation artist and Station X CEO Grant Boucher. "Six people can be given brushes, oil paints, and canvas. But the person who is a trained artist is going to create an image. Everyone else is going to slop it around a bit. If you really want to do film work, you've got to take some filmmaking and art classes. You can learn the tool and the new software, but you still need to have the artistic skill to make use of the tool set. If you don't know the difference between an image that is over lit and under lit, then how are you suppose to do high-end effects work? So, I would recommend both the art classes and the computer classes. If you take just technology classes, you'll be nothing but a technologist who's stumbling with the art. If you're only an artist, it will take you quite a long time to catch up with the technology. Those two areas must work together."

Right brain / Left brain

"I think that the people who survive the cycles of the industry the best are at two extremes," says Rhythm & Hues Vice President and

Co-owner Pauline Ts'o. "One is the ultra specialist, who is the absolute best in some niche position - really tops. The other extreme is the ultra generalist - the one who is excellent in many different areas. There are different levels of generalizing and specializing, but someone who can program as well as be an excellent artist is obviously a stronger candidate than someone who can just draw or just program. And in particular, in actually doing shots and being responsible for shots, you really need both. If you're in the design department, you might not need the technical end. But as a technical director or computer animator, the more you can master a tool - and that means having both aesthetic and technical skills - then the more valuable you're going to be. Finding the people who are truly excellent on both sides of their brain is always difficult. The American public school system is not set up to train both sides of the brain. We're asked to decide - at what I would consider a very early age - between one or the other. And our industry suffers for that. If you're inherently a technical person, don't ignore your artistic side and vice versa. Force yourself to think in that other pattern of thinking. The more you do, the easier it becomes. The percentage of people coming in the studio door with that right-brain, left-brain training is about two percent. And that's what we're always looking for."

Choosing a school

There are plenty of great schools - both college and trade - that teach courses on animation, filmmaking, art design, and other related studies. When studio personnel were asked which schools seemed to turn out students with consistently good skills and demo reels, several came to mind: California Institute of Arts (CalArts), Valencia, CA; Ohio State University-Department of Art & Design, Columbus, OH; Ringling School of Art & Design, Sarasota, FL; Savannah College of Art & Design, Savannah, GA; Sheridan College, Oakville, Ontario, Canada; and Texas A&M University, College Station, TX.

Choosing a school involves weighing many factors, and the few mentioned above (along with those listed in the back of this book) are not intended to be an all inclusive list, or suggest any kind of endorsement. Many schools are actively pursued by studios looking to recruit personnel. Contact the school of your choice to learn what courses and technological support they offer, and whether they participate in any recruitment programs.

Teaching Yourself

A self-taught animation course may be easier to fit into an already busy schedule, but the task of disciplining your time can be daunting to a lot of people. If you have the moxy for a self-taught course, you'll find you can work at your own pace (without giving up your current job), pursue those areas that interest you most, and fine-tune your skills at an accelerated pace (time permitting, of course). The downside of self-instruction is that you'll need to buy a computer capable of professional work, and won't have the luxury of turning to instructors or other students when faced with a problem. When it comes to job hunting, you'll find yourself all alone again. Still, the rewards are great, and for many self-instruction may be the only alternative. You may find it inspiring to know that most of the people running today's boutique studios learned their skills on their own!

Seek out resources around you

Determining which path is right for you depends on where you are geographically. Take advantage of the resources that are available in your area.

"If there's a community college nearby," advises freelance animation director and instructor Brad Carvey, "and they have an incredible program with a $10 million dollar computer lab, then go there. If there is a great art school in your area, you should go there. If there is a great film school in your area, you should definitely go there. You may be isolated to the point where you've got to learn it yourself, and then you should do what I do. When you're working on a computer and waiting around for something to render, study traditional animation, art, compositing, and filmmaking."

Get hands-on training

Whether you choose a trade school or a self-taught course, the most important consideration is hands-on training. You need to be able to spend hours (and hours) with your hands on the keyboard. Watching someone else operate the machine doesn't teach you anything - except that it looks easy!

How many people do you know that learned how to play a musical instrument by watching someone else? It can't be done. I took up piano a few years ago. I would sit down everyday and plunk out notes at an excruciatingly slow pace. If I missed a day, I would regress a week. But once I disciplined myself to play a few minutes everyday, my skill level improved. I began to amaze myself, and my confidence grew. I soon found myself at the keyboard for hours at a time, and saw my skill level grow proportionally. My ability increased in direct relation to my familiarity with the keyboard. Playing music became comfortable, almost *second nature*.

Becoming skilled at computer animation works exactly the same way. It's not enough to know *what* to do (although that is paramount). You'll need to be able to execute your ideas without struggling with *how* to do it. The computer's interface must become as familiar as that piano keyboard. You need to be able to reach for the correct pull-down menu, slider bar, or numeric input without thinking about it. *To become successful in this business, your use of the computer must become* **second nature**.

I'll guarantee you, your competition operates that way. And if your ability with a computer is anything less than second nature, you won't last six months. That's just the way it is.

Everyone feels intimidated by computers. Conquering those fears is as simple as taking one step at a time.

"Learning computer animation is a lot like learning to speak a foreign language," says freelancer Brad Carvey. "You learn a word like 'wasser,' which is German for 'water.' When you visit Germany and you say 'wasser' you'll notice they bring you a glass with water in it. After five or six times, you not only remember the word because it's easy, you also know it works. So now, you've added something to your German tool kit. Now, it's not hard to learn that word. It's just that there's lots of the words you've got to learn. And so, if you learn a little bit at a time, eventually you start to ask for 'cold' water. And then you order a meal. Next, you ask somebody what time it is. It's not hard to learn those individual phrases and words, it's just that you have to stay with it, and eventually you learn to become fluent. And then something magical happens. You learn enough that you become *creative*. Soon, you're adding humor, puns and all the rest to your speech.

"Almost anything that has to do with computers is exactly like that. The computer as a whole is hard to learn, just like it's hard to become fluent and articulate in German. But, any *one* word is easy. So anything that you can learn that's related to film, television, art, lighting, compositing, or software is kind of like another 'word.' You always want to keep incrementally adding to your knowledge until one day you'll have the 'Ah-ha' experience, where you say, 'Oh! I get this!' At that point you can start being creative."

Put in the time *now* to learn the trade, and you'll always be in demand. Remember, most people are unwilling to do what it takes to be at the top.

Chapter 2:
Software and Hardware

I remember my first 3D animation program - *Sculpt 4D*. The interface was confusing and the manual terribly intimidating. I was a novice, with a capital *N*. But, I plowed ahead, struggling with the concepts of points, polygons, and the Cartesian coordinate system. In a few hours I figured out how to make a cube - a rather primitive object. It took my computer - with a whopping one megabyte of RAM - sixteen hours to render the surface of the cube. That's not terribly impressive by today's standards. But, that's where desktop technology was when I got started.

I've worked with quite a few different programs since those early days, and as anyone with experience will tell you - once you understand one 3D program, the rest are pretty much the same. The key for a beginner is to just get started! Take *action*!

You'll want to get a robust 3D animation program and a computer capable of handling all of its features.

You may hear how animation companies prefer to train their employees on their own proprietary animation systems. You'll hear that traditional animation skills are more important than specific computer skills. That's true. Some major studios have special computer animation systems set up that are not commercially available. If you land a job there, you'll need to learn the way they do things.

This leads many newcomers to ask, "Why should I learn computer skills, when I'll need to be retrained on the job?" The answer is simple: Traditional animation skills are essential, but computer skills will get you the job. After all, you want to be a *computer* animator, right? Your mission is to *prove* your abilities in that role. You'll need time on a computer system - your own or one at school - to do that. Many of the concepts of computer animation translate to all systems. You'll need to thoroughly understand those concepts before you can get your foot in the door.

Think you can get by without computer skills? Some studios *have* found it easier to take an artist already well skilled in the art of animation, and teach them how to apply their talent through a computer. It doesn't always work, though.

While working at Will Vinton Studios a few of the "claymation" artists transferred into the computer department to flex their animation muscle with the new technology. Within a few weeks all but one had returned to the more traditional approach. They just couldn't work as fast or as easily as they were accustomed to. The problem was the computer interface. These very skilled animators found themselves struggling to apply their talents using a method that was brand new to them. They failed because they lacked computer skills, not because they weren't great animators. Get computer skills. You'll need them in this business.

What's the best 3D software to learn?

Ideally, you want to master an animation program that the pros are using. In the past, this was impossible because most studios were not using off-the-shelf software. But times change, and now you'll find many major studios using the same software you can buy for home use. The reason is simple: money.

It's cheaper to add a computer running Windows NT (about $3,500), than it is to add a Silicon Graphics workstation (about $15,000). By the time you read this, it'll be even less expensive.

A few of the top animation packages being utilized by the major studios include Softimage, Maya, and LightWave 3D. The most affordable of these is LightWave 3D ($1,995). A light version, called Inspire, runs about $495 dollars.

Less expensive 3D software (Ray Dream 3D, etc.) can be found in the $130 to $300 dollar range, but its very unlikely you'll find a major studio using them.

"We have seen demo reels that are created with those low cost packages," says Foundation Imaging's P.J. Foley, "but so far none of those people have a job here. (laughs) It's not that it can't be done, its just that users are not exploiting the capabilities of those programs as much as they could."

Target your software skills

Although software skills are generally translatable between packages, it helps to know the software being used at your targeted facility.

"Right now we're pretty much interested in people who have some Maya experience," says Metrolight Studios production head, John Follmer. "In the past, when there weren't as many animators available, we would actually train people. But honestly, if you're a great character animator, or if you're great at color and lighting, it's not going to take you much time to come up to speed on a new software. So, in reality, if you have the skills in a fairly high-end software, you're going to be able to translate those skills into another software package very quickly. In the final analysis, we're a financially driven industry. Most studios are focusing on the candidates that already know, or have some experience, with the software currently being used at that facility."

If you don't have a specific studio in mind, target your learning based on what part of the industry you'd like to work in.

"If I was going to pick one piece of high-end software to know, I'd pick Renderman," advises Digital Muse effects supervisor Matt Merkovich. "You'll need to go to school for that. You can use whatever front end you want. If you like Maya, use Maya. If you like Softimage, or Houdini, use that. But use some piece of software that integrates well with Renderman if you want to be working on high-end, motion picture stuff. If you want to work in episodic television or commercials, learn LightWave. But, if you want to work in high-end, big budget, motion picture effects, learn Renderman."

At high-end effects facilities, it's less about the software you know, and more about the operating system.

"Large studios like ours like to see some UNIX experience because that's what we use," says Pauline Ts'o of Rhythm & Hues. "So, it's not so much the particular graphics package, but the operating system environment that you're working in. Packages that let you script plugins - that let you exercise your linear problem solving skills are the ones that we place more emphasis on, because that's what you've got to do when you've got a shot to finish. You've got to breakdown your task in a logical manner. And those types of programs give you more experience doing that. Simply *using* a program that includes the ability to customize settings is not enough. We lean toward people who have actually *made use* of those options."

If your budget forces you to work from home, don't worry. Inexpensive animation software packages *will* teach you the basics.

"Whatever package you use, you could probably get a job anywhere with it," offers Digital Muse creative director Bruce Branit, "as long as you've got the ability to put something on the screen that is visually interesting. If you can do that with a real basic program, a company will take a chance on you because they know that you've got what it takes even if you don't have the best tools at the beginning."

What kind of computer?

After deciding on a software package, you'll need a machine to run it on. The animation software will dictate how robust your computer needs to be. There are a million-and-one possible configurations and dozens of companies capable of putting together a decent machine. I won't try to sort them all out for you here, but I can pass along a few tips I've gleaned from ten years of computer buying:

(1.) **Get only what you think you'll use in the next two years.** Hardware changes every 18 months and software upgrades come at six month intervals. That means, whatever you buy today will be a doorstop in two years. It'll run fine for ten years - you'll just want something better in two, especially when you find out that you can get a machine that's twice as fast at half the price you paid.

(2.) **Put the majority of your money into RAM, hard drive space, and a good monitor.** Animation programs are memory hungry. After two years of upgrades, you'll wish you had twice the RAM. Same goes for hard drive space. You can never have enough of either. Believe me, you'll use it. Most important of all, get a BIG monitor. You don't want to be squinting at a pea-size monitor eight hours a day. When you trade up on a new machine, you can always keep your jumbo-size monitor. Invest in a good one, up front. When buying a stereo system, experts say to put two-thirds of your total system cost into the speakers. That's because the finest system in the world won't be worth the expense if you can't hear it. The same holds true for a computer. The monitor is your window into the computer world. Don't sink all your money into a system and skimp on the monitor. My best recommendation is a system with a minimum of 128 MB of RAM, 10 GB of hard drive space, and a 20-inch monitor.

(3.) **Pay cash.** If you need to take out a loan to get started (like I did), get one that you can pay off in 24 months. Remember, in two years you'll want a new machine, and you don't want to be paying on something that's outdated. Look for a loan written as a lease, with option-to-buy. The interest on these loans can be lower than most, and 100% of your monthly payment is tax deductable.

In addition to the computer, you'll need a playback device that allows you to compile and study your animated creations. One of the best devices on the market is Digital Processing Systems' (DPS) Perception Video Recorder ($1,995). It allows you to string together a series of animated clips when you're ready to show off your best work. The board has video outputs which allow you to dump the sequences to tape for an instant demo reel.

All totaled, you should be able to put together a terrific animation system (including basic software) for about $5,000 dollars.

Just to put that into perspective, I paid more than $20,000 dollars for a similar system in the mid-nineties. (Ouch!) That was a bargain, though. Five years earlier, that same system cost $250,000 dollars. (Yikes!)

Anyway you look at it, it's serious money. But then, you're *serious* about being an animator, right? Whatever your ambition, don't let the cost of getting started prevent you from realizing your dreams. I've talked with plenty of would-be animators who see the cash outlay as an obstacle. "I just don't earn that much," they tell me. Well frankly, nobody does. I sold my extensive record collection at three consecutive garage sales to raise enough money to buy my first computer. You'll find that when you want something bad enough, you'll do whatever it takes to make it happen.

How quick can I expect to get up to speed?

When I got started, I was working a forty-hour week, full time. About eight o'clock every night, I settled in for a few hours at the keyboard, poring through the animation manual and trying my hand at a few tutorials. Most nights I worked at it until midnight. Sometimes, later. After about six months, I was proficient enough that I thought I could sell my work - and did!

Will you follow the same schedule? That's difficult to say. There are a lot of factors involved, not the least of which is how much time you're willing to dedicate to the task of learning a new skill.

When you're first starting out, you'll find that too many hours at the computer screen doesn't really pay off with increased retention. That's because your brain can only absorb so much new information each day. You're better off to plan on at least an hour a day, and see what happens. Many times, I've gone in with an hour in mind and emerged four hours later wondering where the time had gone.

Pace yourself. Start slowly and build a foundation of knowledge. You'll find yourself spending more time, as your ability to retain information increases.

Getting up to speed requires self-discipline, and lots of it. You need to spend a minimum of one hour a day boning up on your animation skills. Whatever you do, *don't skip a day in your first few months*. That includes weekends. You must put in at least an hour a day, until the basics become second nature. (Remember the piano example?) Then, you'll find you can miss a day, return, and pick up where you left off without taking two or three steps backward in the learning process. Ignore this advice, and you'll be doomed to a long and painful learning curve.

On the other hand, if you put in the hours on a regular basis, you should be capable of producing sellable work within four to six months. Assuming you continue to push and stretch your creative abilities, you could easily be one of the top animators in your area within a few years!

Where do I get advice?

The best thing you can do is find a mentor - someone working in your chosen field who's willing to help you. You'd be surprised how many working animators are willing to help you get your act together - just ask! Here's a couple of suggestions so that you don't turn into a pest:

(1.) **Try it yourself, first!** Nothing is more aggravating to a professional than to have their time wasted. Although there is no such thing as a stupid question, you will be expected to exhaust every possible solution to your problem before leaning on your mentor. Don't use your mentor as a crutch. If you find yourself reaching for the phone every time you encounter a problem, you're abusing the relationship. Stockpile your mentor's approaches. Learn to apply the same approaches to each problem. If you're still stuck - contact your mentor, and be prepared to tell them everything you've already tried.

(2.) **Don't waste time.** Get right to the point, and take notes. Don't expect your mentor to hang on the phone while you try their suggestions.

Words of Warning

Never take advice from people who are not where you want to be. This might sound somewhat simplistic, but you'd be surprise how many people let unqualified persons steal their dream. It's easy to get excited about being a computer animator, and you should! But, don't be surprised when you hear friends and family say:

"What do *you* know about computers?"

"I knew someone that tried that and they failed."

"Too bad you didn't get in on the ground floor."

"That'll take years of training."

Your friends and family mean well when they plant these seeds of doubt. But, let's face it - what do *they* know about computer animation? If you wanted to be a baker, would you take advice from the butcher? Of course not! Always qualify those who hand out free advice. You'll find that deep down inside most people want to see you fail. It's not so much that they care whether you do or not. It's just that they are trying to protect their own egos. To many people, your success reminds them of their own missed opportunities. In a twisted sort of way - if you succeed, they fail. Remember:

Never take advice from people who are not where you want to be.

Chapter 3:
Demo Reels

This is your ticket to landing work in the animation business. In the next few pages, you'll learn what it takes to put together a demo reel that will stand out from the hundreds of reels submitted to studios every month.

Understanding the review process

The first thing you need to understand is that *nobody* in the industry has time to look at your demo reel - even when they're under the gun to fill a vacancy.

I've worked in three media related industries in the past twenty-five years and the situation is identical in all three. Time is valuable, and any available free moments are gobbled up with personal relaxation. Invariably, viewing demo reels is put off until the last minute. Most of them demonstrate skill levels well below what is necessary, which makes the process particularly painful. Still, a new hire is needed and so the reviewer plows ahead hoping to discover that one magical candidate who will put an end to the ceaseless parade of really bad demo reels. Occasionally, a fellow animator wanders into the viewing room, and the reviewer asks, "Do you know anybody?" The hope is that an incredibly talented candidate will fall into their lap and put them out of their misery. (Now, you know why most jobs are filled from within an organization.) More than not, the animator replies, "Nobody I could recommend," and the search goes on.

Look at it from their point of view. The reviewer has two missions to accomplish: He's got to find a candidate with the right skill level, and more important, *that person has got to make the reviewer look good*. If the reviewer recommends a person who ultimately fails in the role, the reviewer looks bad.

Therefore, it's very important to make the right choice. The reviewer's ego, credibility, and job are all on the line. The reviewer is looking for someone who is a low risk for potential disaster.

Tips to get your demo reel noticed

Here are some tips to help ensure you've got a reel that will knock their socks off:

(1.) **Focus on your strengths.** If your character animation is top drawer, make sure there is plenty on your reel. If compositing visual effects into live background plates is your stock in trade, showcase it. If lighting, texturing, or modeling is your forte, highlight it. Make sure your reel concentrates on whatever your best at.

"We're always looking for people who are going to fit into one of four categories," says Blue Sky Studios animator Doug Dooley. "Is this person a modeler, an animator, a technical director or a compositor? We look for a skill set that specializes in one of those areas. We look for that to stand out on the reel. It has to be close to the level that we're use to doing here, so that we know that the person can come in rather quickly and start animating on our commercials. Make sure you have a strength in at least one area. In my demo reel, I had absolutely awful lighting. But, animation was obviously my focus. I have student advisors and I always tell them, 'Don't rush the decision, because then you can get trapped.' Some people get in as a technical director, but they really wanted to be an animator. Or the reverse. And then they get trapped, and it's really hard to move over into another specialty at a large studio. So, don't rush the decision. But if you already know you enjoy one specific thing, then make sure you've devoted the greatest portion of your time towards making that area look the best - whether it's animation, lighting, modeling, or compositing."

"If a student wants to do character animation," says freelance animator Brad Carvey, "and that's what he gets *really* excited about, they should do a character animation demo reel and nothing else. Then submit that only to character companies. If they see themselves getting a job in corporate America doing A/V stuff, then do flying logos and that's it. I feel that it's too difficult for someone who's going to school to do a comprehensive demo reel. Over the course of five semesters, I teach six classes at a local junior college. And I see some real talented students. Every semester you get two or three that you *know* are good enough to work anywhere. You know they have everything necessary; that if they could just get hired and get to work, they'll be great. But what happens is they start putting a demo reel together and it looks like crap. And the problem is they don't have time. So, I think it's important to focus the time they do have on their strengths."

"We've had a few demo reels in here where people have recreated shots from movies," says Foundation Imaging's John Allardice. "That's a perfectly valid thing. All this stuff about, 'Don't put spaceships on your reels,' that's bull. The hard and fast rule about not putting spaceships on your reel because most companies will turn your tape off - is *rubbish*. What they're used to seeing are tons and tons of really *bad* spaceships. So, that's where that fable came from. If you can do great spaceships, put them on there. If you can do good character animation, put it on there. Never put something on your reel that you feel you have to, because if you didn't enjoy doing it chances are it's going to suck. Put on the stuff you *love* doing because that will shine through in the way you've put the scene together. It'll show in the final result."

Remember, your demo reel is your ticket in the door. Stack the deck in your favor, by focusing on your strengths. Here's a rundown on some of the job descriptions and what employers are looking for in a demo reel:

(a) **Character animator.** Make sure your characters are original and emote personality. A common mistake is to concentrate too much on the modeling and lighting instead of the character animation. Studios would much rather see a very simple, quick shaded model rather than one that is fully modeled and rendered. Concentrate on the *performance,* and don't confuse *motion* with character animation. Character animation is about acting. Create a personality. It's not just a matter of applying principles of squash & stretch, anticipation, overlapping action, and follow through. The character's personality should drive *how* those things are accomplished. That's what gives the character personality. It's a common mistake for animators to stop at the first level. Showing perfect walk cycles (weighted, natural walks that avoid sliding feet) is not enough at most studios. Having your character do something that's funny, serious, or interesting is preferred.

(b) **Modeler.** Include plenty of examples of complex and intricately designed models. For example, some studios look for at least one bevel between two planes to add a little bit of detail. You should submit examples of both mechanical and organic objects. Organic objects are the toughest to create, and therefore grab the attention of employers. Surfacing the models (rather than just wireframes) is a plus. Although stills of your creations are fine, an animated model shows off your work in motion! Ultimately, that's the goal, right?

(c) **Technical Director.** Show off your ability to balance light and color. Create dimensional sets and light them in various ways to establish mood and emotion. A common mistake is trying to use all sixteen million colors available on the computer. Go back to basic art principles and understand what a limited color palette can do for you. Avoid lighting scenes in one of two extremes - everything ambient, or everything black with just a few spotlights. In reality, most of the world is in between. Create a collection of custom textures. Apply them to objects in your lighting schemes. A common mistake is using a texture map that looks pretty good far away, but looks plastic up close. Put a little motion to the camera (no flying cameras, please!) to emphasize the dimensional qualities of your sets.

(d) **Game Modelers/Animators.** Create characters and objects with low polygon counts. Apply custom textures, and emphasize your ability to milk the most out of low polygonal models, while retaining a realistic look. Focus on organic models, rather than robots and machinery.

(2.) **Target your prospective employer.** The needs of boutique animation houses are different than those of the major studios. Most of their work involves flying logos and visual effects for television. Character animation skills - although appealing - don't find much use at these shops. Even the majors have specialized needs. Industrial Light & Magic (ILM) looks for reels with visual effects. Pixar seeks terrific character animators. Digital Domain prefers reels showing animation composited with live action. Disney and Warner Brothers want to see tradition cel animation, as well as computer character skills. Make sure you know what the needs are of the facility that you're applying to. Construct your reel so that it appeals to *their* needs.

"If you're just starting out, target your demo reel," advises Matt Merkovich, an effects supervisor with Digital Muse. "Figure out where you want to work, what kind of work you want to do, and keep in mind it's show business and not everyone wants to see or do giant fighting robots. They'll look at it once, shelve it, and that'll be the last you hear from them. If you want to work in commercials, pick a commercial you like and try to duplicate it. Then send that out to commercial post effect facilities and you'll get a job. It's that simple. Just make sure your reel displays a level of competence comparable to the effects work being done at the facility you're trying to get hired at. That's very important. If you don't feel you are competent enough to do a *Star Trek* effects shot, two things should occur to you. First, maybe you're not ready to work at a company that does effects for *Star Trek*, and second, maybe you should target your demo reel at facilities that match your current level of ability. For instance, maybe there is a facility that does fabulous flying chrome logos and that's what you do really well. That's where you should be applying. Get a job in the industry that suits your talents, then develop your skills from there. A year down the road, you can put together a dynamite effects reel and submit it to the effects facility of your choice. All you have to do is put four shots that total thirty seconds on a tape and send it to me with a note that says, 'I did these four shots because they seem to be the kind of shots that your facility does. I'm interested in working with you. Call me if you're interested. PS. It took me two weeks to do these four shots.' From that information, I can gauge how good you can be."

John Allardice, a supervising visual effects animator at Foundation Imaging looks to see if a candidate is trying to tell a story. "I look for some filmmaking ability there - knowing when to cut, and what to cut to. That doesn't apply at a lot of houses - it does apply here. We've had a couple of reels in recently in which the surfacing wasn't great, modeling wasn't perfect, and the rendering wasn't top notch. But, they did know how to tell a story with the camera and with the characters within the shot. They knew how to block. They knew how to make something funny. Don't be impressed by the fact that you got something to move from *A* to *B* in your reel. I mean, yea, all your mates might be slapping you on the back and saying, 'Yea, that's great.' But, when it comes down to it, take out a TV show with some effects in it and say, 'Could I cut my stuff into that?' If the answer is no, go back and do some more work on your reel. Because, no house can really afford to bring somebody in and train them. We need to be able to sit someone down - not in the first day, but within a week or so - and they've got to be cranking out stuff we can use.

There's *no* downtime in this business, especially in episodic television. You have to be at the sort of level where you'd be happy to see your reel cut into a show."

Animators need to keep in mind that visual effects studio's like Foundation Imaging want work that will cut in well with their own.

"What Foundation is trying to do is resell an animator's work as our own," explains supervising animator Jeff Scheetz. "We've got a look that people have come to expect from us, and a candidate's work has to look like it came out of here, because once we give them a desk and a computer they've got to create work that lives up to founder Ron Thornton's reputation. So, look at what's coming out of the professional houses and try to be critical of your own work to see if it meets that standard. Try to figure out where lights are positioned and why. Then try to reproduce that in your own work. Know that it is not necessarily an originality contest, or a short film contest, or anything else. It is - essentially - a demonstration of technical abilities that we will come to count on in the future should we hire you. *Never* let anyone tell you what should or shouldn't be on your demo reel. You should do what you're passionate about. If you love spaceships, do spaceships and send them to a company that does spaceships. If you love squash and stretch character animation, find a company that does that and try to get a job there. When you're not doing the kind of work you like, you're probably not going to be a very happy."

Studios that specialize in character animation, like Rhythm & Hues, are looking for a strong grasp of those fundamentals.

"We look for the basic fundamentals of animation - timing, squash and stretch, performance - all of that stuff," explains Rhythm & Hues' Lyndon Barrois. "And you can tell immediately if someone has that skill - how to give weight to a character, how to make a character think, and how to show it's alive. It's different from just making something move across the screen. Whether its hand drawn, computer generated, stop motion - it doesn't matter. We look to see if you have an understanding of the skill and the fundamentals of character animation. It's not so important that you have computer skills when you come into a studio, because that's just a tool. Anybody can learn how to use it. I had none when I came here. All of my animation was stop motion. I took my first semester at Cal Arts and took all of the fundamentals of 2D animation - how to make things move with drawings. I applied all of that to my stop motion animation. That's all I did for the three years I was at Cal Arts. Even my freelance work was stop motion."

Keep in mind that large studios and smaller boutique studios are looking for different things.

"Big companies look for people to specialize more than smaller companies," advises Pauline Ts'o of Rhythm & Hues. "As a big company, we do look for a demonstration of high excellence in at least one area, and we would rather take someone that clearly shows just high excellence in, say, modeling; versus someone that shows an average skill in all the areas. So, structure the reel to cater to your strength."

"As a smaller animation house, we tend to favor new hires who display a combination of abilities," says executive producer Jeff Barnes of Computer Cafe. "I'll give you an example. We recently hired a young man who had been on LightWave for about a year. No national experience, but he had done some pieces he had made up at home while he was going to school. One was a broadcast logo, one was a character animation piece, and one was a photoreal environment piece. He only had three or four pieces on his reel. But all of those were extremely strong. I'll bet the reel was under two minutes. When we brought him here for an interview, he had exceptional illustration skills, so we knew the guy had a great eye. He was an artist. Beyond that he was very technically oriented. He had taken some computer classes in college and he understood the computer - not to a huge degree. But, he definitely showed he had an aptitude for it. So, in a lot of ways he was the perfect example of the kind of person we hire."

Many production companies have web sites detailing what they're looking for in new hires. If you don't find what you're looking for on-line, call them and ask!

(3) **Keep it short.** How short? I've heard suggestions that reels should be no longer than three to five minutes. Frankly, that's far too long. The average demo reel gets about ten seconds before a decision is made on whether to continue or not. Sounds brutal, doesn't it? But, it's the truth.

Each year, the major studios accept tapes and resumes from would-be animators at ACM's annual SIGGRAPH convention. These "cattle-calls" draw hundreds of demo tapes. These huge numbers are whittled down to the top one hundred or so, through an on-site interview process. The remaining tapes are taken back to the studio, where a board of on-staff animators take their shots. Having sat in on a few of these sessions, I can tell you that most of the comments weren't very kind. People like to tear apart demo reels, even if they like them. They'll say, "Oh look, he doesn't know how to use anti-aliasing. Oh, look at that. He should have used this," or "He did that wrong." But, a lot of times the criticism that you hear is just people trying to prove that they're noticing things. As you might expect, there is a lot of personality issues that come into play in these sessions. Although it would be nice to think that everyone's professional and can view these tapes objectively, that's not always the case. In these group situations, peer pressure can play a big role in determining who likes what, and why. I've seen terrific animations ripped on by young animators, who suddenly do an about-face when a senior player stands up and properly compliments the work. I suppose some get a feeling of power when they're put in the position of sitting in judgment of someone else's work. Right or wrong, it's the way the world works, and you'd better build a tight reel if you hope to survive this kind of gauntlet.

The best way to do that is to keep your demo reel short and focused. How short? I've seen terrific reels that were less than sixty seconds! But, I think ninety-seconds to two-minutes is more than enough. First of all, the reviewers will never get passed the first ten-seconds if you don't grab them. In that case, a two to five-minute demo reel is a waste. If you manage to hold their attention in the opening ten-seconds, the reviewers will probably watch the next thirty to sixty-seconds. If you've still got them at the end of that period, they'll watch the remainder of your reel. You don't want it too long. Ideally, they want to see more of your work when your name and telephone number pop up at the tail. Secondly, it's extremely difficult (if not impossible!) for a beginning animator to sustain a five minute demo reel with quality work.

The best way to keep your reel short is to include *only* your best shots. Be critical. Don't include a history of your career and abilities. No one is interested in how you've improved over the years. Show them where your skills are *today*.

"Not only can you judge someone's ability by looking at a reel," adds Digital Muse creative director Bruce Branit, "but you can judge what they *think* of their ability by looking at their reel. If they put a lot of pretty good things on a reel and then some absolutely awful things on there, then it might be that they don't know which of their stuff is good or bad. I would rather have a reel that is thirty seconds long, than a reel that is a minute long with thirty seconds of crap. There's a general attitude that *a reel is as good as it's worst element.*"

Remember, never pad your reel to a predetermined length. Include only your best work. Let the content determine the final length.

(4.) **Follow the format.** Every reel should follow the basic format that reviewers are expecting to see. Don't try to get cute with a big build up (a John Smith Production, of a Digital Studios Creation, of a...etc.) hoping this will make your reel stand out (it will, but it won't get you any favorable reviews!). Keep it simple and cut to the chase. Here's a brief lineup of what should appear on the reel:

(a) **Your Name and Phone Number.** This goes at the head and tail of the reel. Don't make the reviewer look for it. A still is fine, but you're an animator, aren't you? Make it move, but keep it short and to the point. Dazzle them, don't bore them. Running length: 5 seconds.

(b) **Your best shot.** Give them your best effort - best character animation, best visual effect, best composite work - right here. This should be the most outstanding example you've got. Running length: 5-10 seconds.

(c) **More of your best work.** String together a sequence of animation work. Better to weight your reel with similar shots or techniques. If you need to, build a separate reel to showcase each of your multiple talents. Keep the shots as short as possible (3-5 seconds each). Rather than show a lengthy shot, pick out the most interesting three to five second clip and use it. A string of shots like this (joining the action in progress, and cutting out before the action ends) will convey that your reel is just a *sample*, and you have much more to offer! Running length: 30-60 seconds

Cut this montage to music for best effect. Music will improve the feel of your reel immeasurably. Sound effects are great, but not absolutely necessary. Use music that is upbeat and friendly. Avoid popular songs (heavy metal, rap, punk, disco, etc.). Everybody uses them! After looking at a hundred reels, your reviewer will be looking for an excuse not to view yours. Don't give them one! Use an instrumental selection, preferably pulled from a "needle drop" collection. These are timed music cuts (30, 60, and 90-seconds) that can be found at most post-production houses. Price is based on a per-use charge, per cut - usually under $50 dollars. Whatever you do, don't over cut your reel.

"Don't edit your reel like you're applying to work at MTV," warns Grant Boucher of Station X. "We want to see what you can do. If we only see eight frames of each shot, we'll never have a concept of what you're capable of doing. When we edit our studio demo reel, it contains nice long cuts of the effects work we've done. We're proud of our work and want to show it off. The same thing goes when you're sending us work. Each shot needs to be long enough for us to judge your capabilities."

The best approach is to find a music track that closely fits the tempo of your existing shot sequence. Then, make slight adjustments to the image sequences until you get a match. Let the shot sequence dictate the music selection.

"Before you edit your reel, take the time to look at other reels to see what constitutes a good editing job," recommends Digital Muse's Matt Merkovich. "We get reels that have a fifteen second shot of someone's name flying up very slowly to the camera, and then the words 'demo reel' bounce out very nicely, and I'm thinking, 'Okay. I know it's your demo reel because you sent it to me.' You don't need to put these long unnecessary things in there. We're interested in the type of work that we do at this facility. Show us that kind of work. I'd rather see thirty seconds of really good work than four minutes of junk. That's where editing comes in. Keep it tight. Don't put long running shots on the reel - unless there is a reason for it. If you did this long sequence - like the opening for the movie *Contact* - cut it up before you put it on the reel. I'll think, 'Oh! You did the opening for the movie *Contact*. Moving right along...' In fact, don't worry about your reel being too short. Worry about the quality of the content."

(d) **Your Name and Phone Number.** This can be the same slate you used at the head of the reel. Sell yourself! Let them see your name and phone number again. Then, fade to black. Running length: 5 seconds.

Most reels can end here. But if you've worked on some broadcast commercials or big projects, add the following:

(e) **Full productions.** If some of the shots you featured above were taken from a commercial spot or team project, include the spot here with its original soundtrack. This gives the reviewer a chance to see how your shot fit into the whole, or in many cases, just a chance to be entertained by a cool animated spot they may have missed. Letting them know you worked on a national spot or team project doesn't hurt either! No need to repeat your name and phone number again. Just fade to black.

(5.) Keep your packaging simple and professional. Packaging is a lot more important than most people think it is. It not only says a lot about your professionalism, but it can help keep your demo reel at the fingertips of your prospective employer. There are some obvious tip-offs to amateur demo reels. Avoid them, if you hope to be considered:

(a) **Use hardcases instead of cardboard sleeves.** You can get plastic hardcases (.50 cents each) at a videotape supply house in your area. They look nicer, and protect your submission while it's in the mail. Order the cases with the full window - its a plastic sleeve on the outside of the case that holds a label or cover design. Use the sleeve to hold a cover design that includes stills from some of your work.

"When I put all the demo reels on my shelf," says Foundation Imaging's Jeff Scheetz, "and I want to get my hands on somebody, I can look at cover art and say, 'I remember exactly who this is.' I'll still consider a person who scrawled their name on a piece of masking tape and stuck it on a tape, but their tape might not be as easy to access as a demo tape that has cover art."

The cover design of your hardcase artwork should include your name, phone number, address, email, and other contact information (same as the tape label).

(b) **Use short length tape stock.** Demo reels should be recorded on five minute length VHS videotape. Don't use the 120 minute length tapes from the discount office supply. It's a waste of tape and a sure sign of an amateur. Instead, contact a tape supply house in your area, and order a quantity of five minute length tapes (about $2.50).

U-matic, or three-quarter inch, videotape used to be the professional standard that set you apart from the amateur, but most facilities are getting away from this format and moving toward VHS for viewing dubs. It's simply more convenient. However, you might consider keeping a small supply of three-quarter inch videotape copies of your demo reel on hand, just in case!

Don't reuse tape stock or send old dubs. If your reel has big glitches, drop outs and all kinds of junk running through it, don't send it. In Hollywood there are standards for the quality of work. Don't send something that looks like the cat dragged it in. Spend a buck and get a new tape.

(c) **Label tapes with your contact information.** This includes your name, address, phone number, email, and total running length.

(d) **Include a breakdown of the tape contents.** List each shot contained on the reel. For group projects, shots, and sequences list what role you played. Tape the list on the inside front cover of the hardcase, or include it as part of the back cover art design.

"A resume on the back cover of the demo reel is also a good thing," recommends Foundation Imaging's Jeff Scheetz, "because paper work tends to not follow the reel to the shelf. And that's true at most of the other places where I've seen how people manage the demo reel load."

(e) **Use bubble mailers.** Never use paper pulp mailers. When they rip (as they often do) the pulp padding gets into the tape mechanism and ruins it. The mailer should be big enough (8.5 x 13.5 inches) to comfortably hold your tape and resume.

Demo reel mistakes

Animation studios report a number of common mistakes that beginners make when putting together their demo reels. For many, these errors turn the review process into a "painful" experience.

"We call it 'Theater of Pain' because for the most part the reels are painful to watch," explains executive producer John Gross. "People don't listen to advice on how to do reels. They don't understand the best way to do a reel that will keep people interested, or they don't put their best work on the reel - they put *all* their work on it. Things like that. Some of them are just very painful to get through. If it's *really* horrible - which is pretty rare - but if it is, then we'll just eject it. It's kind of a running joke - but if the tape ends up on my shelf and it hasn't been rewound, we sort of know what happened."

If you hope to be spared from being "ejected," here are things you should *avoid* when creating your reel:

(1.) **Avoid unnecessary details.** "If a ship you modeled is only going to be seen from one side," advises Foundation Imaging's John Allardice, "don't bother detailing the other side of it. (laughs) It's simple stuff like that people tend to forget because they get so wrapped up, 'Oh look at this really cool ship I built.' They never think of how it's going to be used. If you're going to have a character on your reel and you're only going to see it from the waist up, don't build his legs. Some people forget stuff like this. They tend to build for any eventuality. The solution is to *board* your demo reel. Once you create a storyboard, figure out what you don't need to build. You're not wasting time that way. You can get your reel out, and get a job quicker."

(2.) **Never use stock objects.** "I got a demo reel from a student one time that had a beautiful Lifesaver candy animation on it," explains freelance animator Brad Carvey. "He had a pack of Lifesavers modeled and textured that looked great! It had a national or commercial look to the quality of the textures. Then he had some other stuff that included stock models that I recognized from LightWave. So, immediately I didn't know what in the demo reel he had done. As it turns out, he had modeled all the Lifesavers himself. I told him later than when I saw the stock objects, I immediately discounted his honesty and his capabilities. Using stock objects put everything in question."

(3.) **Avoid canned textures.** "Practice as much as you can with all the tools that let you go beyond the canned, push-button effects," recommends Robert Lurye of Rhythm & Hues. "Some people will just take the canned texture that comes with the program and use it as is. And there are people who can recognize that, 'Oh, that's the wood that comes with the demo!' So, here's someone who didn't use any creativity at all and just stuck that on. They could have scanned their own, and come up with something a little different. Those are the hundred of reels that you pretty much throw out right away."

(4.) **Don't loop animations.** "I once got a demo reel of the same animation repeating itself for about twenty minutes," chuckles Brad Carvey. "It was a seven or eight second thing that looped. We watched it for six minutes laughing our heads off. I kept saying, 'It's going to change, I know it's going to change!' Of course, I knew it wasn't. The guy didn't have any title graphics at the beginning and no name on it. That was perhaps one of the stupidest reels we ever got."

(5.) **Never put color bars and tone at the front.** "Color bars and tone are for calibrating equipment," says effects supervisor Matt Merkovich. "At no point do I need to calibrate my audio or video to watch your reel. I know you are trying to look 'professional' by putting bars and tone on your reel, but you don't understand why they're there, and consequently it makes you look amateurish. If you want to put a little academy countdown at the head of the reel so I know when it starts, that's cool. That's actually something I can use."

(6.) **Avoid doing short films.** "I've told students over and over again to avoid short films," warns Metrolight Studios' animator Jeremie Talbot. "A lot of people think that they can pull off a three minute animation while still in school. They'll say, 'Well, it's a *short* story, it's three minutes long.' Well, three minutes is 5,400 frames! I don't think it's possible to do a short film in a semester on a computer because it requires too many resources and too much time. Ultimately, their demo reel will suffer. They'll get parts of the character modeled, and part of it animated, a couple textures here and there - and it just doesn't come together. You're far better off to keep it simple. If you want to do character animation, then figure out a short little piece of dialogue and do that. You can always build on what you've started, but you've got to get the essentials first. The reason I say that is most students bite off more than they can chew. And at the end of their last semester in school, they don't have anything because they haven't finished it. They run out of time."

Chapter 4:
Getting the Job

To get a job in computer animation you need to get the interview. Nobody is hired over the phone. Your mission is to get inside the door and meet with the person doing the hiring.

Investigate

Investigate the marketplace to see what facilities interest you. Do you want to do character animation? Are you interested in motion picture effects? Are you looking for post-production work where you can get your feet wet?

For facilities in your state, call the Office of Film and Television for a copy of their production guide. You'll find a list of production companies, their credits, and contacts listed by category.

For Los Angeles and Hollywood, get a copy of the *Hollywood Reporter Blu-Book* ($65). This spiral bound guide is updated yearly and provides listings for producers, production companies, post production facilities, special effects houses, animation companies, and more.

Libraries are another great source of information. Look for trade magazines like: *Film & Video*, *Post*, *Cinefex* and *Computer Graphics World*. Each has articles and advertisements that will let you know who's doing what in your area of interest.

Prepare a list of facilities that interest you.

First Contact

Telephone each company on your list and find out the name of the person in charge of hiring. Usually it will be the creative director, a supervising animator, or the head of production. Your goal here is to get the name. You'll need it to send your demo reel to the proper person. Without it, your hard work could float around - or worse, find its way to the trash.

Once you've wrangled the name from the telephone receptionist, you want to try to get that person on the telephone. Your goal here is to find out if there are any plans to add staff in the near future. If not, you can file the name for a future contact. If they are looking for a new hire, you can find out more about the position, and let them know to watch the mail for your reel.

Now, as you may have guessed, yours will not be the first call the telephone receptionist has gotten asking these questions. The receptionist's job is to screen and direct calls, and your inquiry call is going to be low on the priority list. You've got to get past the receptionist's desk without getting blown off. Here are some tips to do just that:

(1.) **Ask for the creative director.** Don't ask for the person in charge of hiring. As far as the receptionist knows, you're calling the creative director (CD) to farm out some work to their facility. The nice thing for you is the CD knows all projects currently in production, as well as all potential future projects. Therefore, the CD knows the staffing needs of the facility. If they don't do the hiring directly, they know who does and can direct you.

(2.) **Use a company name.** To weed out inquiry calls, the receptionist will ask for the name of the company you're calling from. Incorporate your own name into your response: John Smith Animation, or Smith Productions. This will give you a better edge than saying, "There is no company," or "It's just John Smith."

(3.) **Be friendly.** Telephone receptionists are not usually afforded the courtesy they deserve. Starting with a friendly, "Good morning! Who is your creative director?," will go a long way toward getting connected. Smile when you talk on the phone. It really does put a spring in your voice.

(4.) **Respond quickly.** This is the key ingredient. It is a fact that *the quickness of your response is more important than what you say.* Think about it. When you're ordering a pizza, your responses are quick and to the point. Why? Because it's *routine*. Your call to the creative director must also sound routine. If you sound nervous and unsure of yourself, you sound like a hundred other inquiry calls. Relax! Try calling the facilities low on your priority list first, and practicing on them. Then, apply your suave skills to the creme de le creme.

Here's what you might expect in a typical call:

Them:	"Digital Animation Productions. How may I help you?"
You:	Good morning! Who's the head of production?"
Them:	"Mike Stephens."
You:	"Is Mike in?
Them:	"Can I say who's calling?"
You:	"John Smith."
Them:	"Your company name?"
You:	"Smith Productions."
Them:	"Just a moment."

Not so hard, right? You'll get thrown a few curve balls as you make your first calls, but don't worry. They get easier the more you do.

Best time to call

The best time to call is in the morning - 9 a.m. to 10 a.m.; early in the week - Monday or Tuesday. The strategy is simple. As the day (and the week) wear on, creative directors and animation supervisors get extremely busy. However, if you can catch them early in the day, before meetings put a stranglehold on their time, you've got a good chance of making contact. Same goes for connecting early in the week. The end of the week tends to be smothered in deadlines. Avoid lunchtimes and late afternoon. Leaving a message in voicemail can blow your shot. Your unfamilar name won't be high on the priority list. Although some good hearted creatives return *all* messages, most just don't have the time. If you continually leave voicemail messages ("Hi, this is John Smith calling again..."), your name will be poison. I've found it's always better to catch them in their office. If you *must* leave a voice message, leave your name and number, but not the purpose of the call. Then, wait three or four days, and try again.

Be brief

When you make contact, get right to the point and be brief. You'll make the best impression if you can get off the phone *before* you're invited to. (You'll know what I mean, when it happens.) Your mission is to find out if they're hiring, who to send a reel to, and when you can expect a response. That's it! Don't try to establish a lifelong friendship. The best way to get points is to *respect the other person's time*. Get off the phone as soon as you can. If you need the correct spelling of a name, or an address change, call back and get it from the telephone receptionist. Don't waste the creative director's time with details that can be found elsewhere.

If the facility is in the same area you are, try to set up a meeting to show your reel personally. This is easier than you think! Tell the creative director you're just letting people in town know what you can do and that you're available. Don't ask about employment. Let them raise the issue. Your mission is to color the meeting as a non-pressure, informational get together. Once there, you'll find *the meeting will become an interview* during which you can deliver all of the information you want your future employer to know. Remember, if you can get inside the door, you're much closer to being hired!

Sending your Demo Reel and Resume

Most animation studios and production houses will ask you to send your demo reel and resume for review. This makes the review process easier for them, but doesn't exactly favor you. Look at it from their point of view. They've got to sift through hundreds of reels and resumes to find a few candidates worth talking to. This task forces them to look for reasons *not to want to talk with you*. If you give them everything they need to make a decision without you, they won't call you for an interview. Remember, you won't get the job if you don't get the interview. *Your goal is to use your demo reel and resume to get the interview*. The only way to do this is to avoid giving them everything they need to make a decision without you. This is accomplished by crafting an introductory cover letter and a one page resume to accompany your demo reel.

Crafting a cover letter

Your cover letter should be no more than two or three paragraphs, of two or three sentences each. Your purpose is simply to explain who you are, what position you're applying for, and what materials are being enclosed. Here's a sample:

Mr. Michael Stephens
Creative Director
Digital Studio Productions
123 Main Street
Anywhere, USA   55555

Dear Mr. Stephens:

Per our telephone conversation this date:

I am most interested in the position of computer animator and welcome the opportunity to talk with you about how I can add value to your staff.

Enclosed you'll find a VHS tape containing examples of my most recent animation work, along with a summary of my background.

I look forward to meeting with you soon.

Best regards,

John Smith

/enclosures

Creating a Resume

There are plenty of terrific books on the market that examine the art of resume writing, and I won't presume to summarize all of the nuances of the craft here. My goal is to show you how to get the interview, and there are certain resume "rules" you'll need to adjust to make that happen. First, your resume should be one page. This is harder than it sounds, even for students fresh out of school who have little experience to relate. Remember, your mission is to give them just enough to want to ask you questions in person, but not enough to make a decision without you. Here's a few tips to get you thinking in the right direction:

(1.) **Focus on animation education.** Include traditional art and animation classes, film study courses, etc. Today's studios are hungry for people with a solid understanding of traditional animation skills. Play these up. If there are examples created during these courses that appear on your demo reel - make note of it. If you landed a degree, mention it. But, don't expect the diploma to carry much weight. The proof will be on your reel. Avoid elementary and high school listings (nobody cares).

(2.) **Leave out dates.** This is the kind of detail that's best left for the interview, *if* anyone is interested. Putting dates on your resume only works against you. Old dates make you look like a has-been, new dates make you look inexperienced.

(3.) **List animation credits.** If you have worked on any project, include it as part of your employment history. If you have not yet worked in the industry, list those jobs that demonstrate your ability to work in teams or manage teams.

At the bottom of the page, type and center in caps: DEMO REEL AND SAMPLES AVAILABLE ON REQUEST. This line nudges the reviewer toward including you in the interview process. The demo reel mentioned could be the one enclosed, or a reel of additional animations. The reference to samples applies to anything you carry under your arm into the interview (i.e. a portfolio of drawings, sketches, and storyboards).

Layout the resume as a single page, with a 12 to 14 point typeface. Don't be afraid to leave a lot of white space. Remember, this page is designed to fulfill their request without giving away the farm. Entice them into giving you an interview!

Resume realities

You should understand going in that the role a resume plays depends on what you're applying for. Resumes are generally secondary when it comes to landing a job as an animator at a studio. Many studios don't even look at them.

"I don't look at resumes," admits Foundation Imaging's Jeff Scheetz. "I look at demo reels. I'll look at a resume after I'm interested in the person. We had a young animator, who was seventeen at the time, come and spend Christmas break with us because he was better than most of the people that we hire. We would have offered him a job, but he had a bright college future ahead of him that he really wanted to pursue. He was self-taught, and his work was excellent. His resume was irrelevant."

"Ultimately, people don't care about your educational background at all," adds Digital Muse effects supervisor Matt Merkovich. "They care about, 'Can you get my job done on time, and have it look the way I want it to look?' If you can say, 'Yes,' and really be able to deliver, then you're golden."

If your coming from a technical degree background - physics degree, mechanical engineering degree, math degree, or computer science degree - studios tend to place more emphasis on your resume.

Second Contact

This is your follow up call to make sure your demo reel got into the right hands. It also gives you an excuse to get your name in front of the creative director again. Allow the CD one week to view your reel, then call. Keep the call brief. "Hi, this is John Smith, and I just called to make sure you got the demo reel I sent." Then, shut up. If your mailing list is on target, you'll get one of three responses:

(1.) **"Yes, but I haven't had a chance to view it."** This is usually what you'll hear. Your response, "Great! I'll look to hear from you soon." Then get off the phone.

(2.) **"Yes, but you're not quite what we need at the moment."**
This is the polite blow off. Ask for a specific suggestion on how
you might improve your reel, then listen. Thank them for their
consideration, and move on to your next prospect.

(3.) **"Yes, I found it very interesting."** This is the one you've been
waiting for. Your response, "Terrific! When can we get together?" Try to
schedule a meeting at the supervisor's earliest convenience, while your
work is still fresh in their mind.

The Interview

There are people that have pretty good demo reels - maybe even
exceptional reels - but have zero people skills. The interview process
helps studios weed through potential candidates and find talented people
who will mesh well with their assembled team. Adding someone who
has horrible communication skills and doesn't get along with people
only introduces a kink into a well oiled machine. Let's face it, no studio
wants that.

"You can tell whether someone is going to fit well or not during the
interview process," says Rhythm & Hues' Lyndon Barrois. "You can tell
when someone's snowballing you. So much comes across in that
process. Unless this person is amazingly talented, their lack of people
skills is going to work against them. As shallow as the skill pool is,
there is always someone out there who you will be able to find to fill any
position you need. Don't forget, there are a lot of hungry, talented people
out there who want to work. Even if they aren't the greatest talent,
personally they're just absolutely fantastic people and you know they
are eager and enthusiastic. And you know that if you plug them in, they
are going to soar. Those are the people you look for."

Meeting with a prospective employer can be a frightening
experience. Even the most successful people find butterflies in
their stomachs as they approach these meetings. However, they
manage to suppress those emotions, and display an air of confidence.
You should too. Here are some suggestions for turning an interview
into a *power* meeting:

(1.) **Use a firm handshake.** First impressions are most important,
and a dishrag handshake will kill your chances quicker than anything.
Grasp the interviewer's hand firmly, and squeeze as you shake. How

hard to squeeze is generally determined by the other party. Match it. Women should not be afraid to do the same. It is considered courteous to allow the woman to offer her hand first. Women that do, display confidence. Most men are reluctant to squeeze a women's hand too hard, so ladies shouldn't read too much into a return handshake that doesn't quite match theirs.

(2.) **Look them in the eye.** When you shake hands, smile and look the interviewer in the eye. Downcast eyes are a sign of weakness. Some people have a particularly hard time returning an eye-to-eye look. Practice before going to the interview. When you talk to people look them directly in the eye. Don't look away until they do. You'll find that most people will cave in and break eye contact first. It may very well be that the interviewer will do the same.

(3.) **Smile.** Nothing is more contagious than a smile. If the interviewer is in a grumpy mood (which won't exactly help your chances), you can turn them around with your pearly whites. Think about all the money you're going to make - that'll really put a smile on your face!

(4.) **Use body language to your advantage.** Body language is of tremendous importance when meeting with people. Hidden thoughts, ideas, and emotions are conveyed to other people everyday through your posture. Most people are unaware of this, but you can take advantage by purposely using body language to influence your interviewer. Before approaching the interview process, read any one of a dozen books on the subject. It'll improve your personal contacts tremendously. Here are just a few insights:

(a) **Keep an open posture.** Crossing your arms or legs during an interview can signal the interviewer that you are a "closed" person. Keep your arms to your sides, or when seated, resting comfortably on the arms of the chair.

(b) **Lean in.** Leaning away from the interviewer suggests a disinterest in the subject. Instead, lean toward the interviewer. Sit on the edge of the chair if necessary. Hang on their every word.

(c) **Nod your head.** Let them know you are listening and understand what they're saying.

(5.) **Ask questions.** Most people sit through an interview as if it's an interrogation. Actually, you should be asking as many questions - *or more* - than the interviewer. How is the organization set up? What kind of hours are involved? What are the chances of advancement? Remember, you're trying to decide whether you want to spend a good portion of your time working for them. Is it going to be worth it? Is taking the job moving you closer to your goal? Your questions let the interviewer know the intensity of your interest. Remember, you're not looking for a handout. You're interested in working for someone who can help you further *your* career goals.

(6.) **Listen.** You'll get the answers to all your questions if you simply take time to listen. Each time you ask a question, stop. *Listen.* Wait until the interviewer has finished. Concentrate on what they are saying, *not on what you're going to say next*. It has often been said that the best conversationalist is the person you listens. When you listen with your whole being - literally hang on every word - you pay the person talking the highest compliment. You're letting them know you find them fascinating! Everyone wants to feel that what they have to say is important. Allow the interviewer to feel that, and you'll be much closer to getting that dream job!

(7.) **Show your latest creations.** Most interviewers will review your demo reel in your presence. This gives you a chance to talk about how you accomplished each sequence. Don't hesitate to sell yourself. People often equate selling themselves with bragging, boasting, arrogance, and other negative emotions. Not true. An honest appraisal of your talents and abilities is a good and *necessary* fact of life. After all, if you don't sell yourself, who will? The only time you'll get into trouble is if you start selling something you're not, or something you can't do. Keep it honest, and you'll excel. Always bring additional samples of work: drawings, storyboards, or animation sequences. Let the interviewer know you have a few new things you're been working on that you'd like to show them. The idea is to convey that you're moving ahead with your career plans - no matter what the interviewer decides. You must exude the cool confidence that you'll land a job sooner or later - it's just a matter of time. Nobody wants to be left behind, and when you show that you're going to be successful with or without them, people have a natural tendency to want to be around you. If you look desperate, or convey that you need this job (true or not), you'll tend to push people away. This is probably hardest thing to do when you're just starting out. The simple fact of the matter is you do *want* the job, and you *need* to get started. The trick is not to let the interviewer see it. Approach the interview like it's one of many offers you're entertaining.

(8.) **Have fun.** Above all, relax! You'll be on many interviews as your career takes shape. Look at each one as a chance to rub shoulders with people in the business, and tour some of best animation studios in the world.

Internships

Perhaps one of the best ways of getting a foot in the door - short of landing a job - is to take a position as an intern. Most studios have an intern program, and I highly recommend taking advantage of them.

"I advise my students to offer to work for free," says veteran animator Brad Carvey. "Just go into any place and try to get an internship for a month and work for free. That's how a lot of people get started. One beginner worked a summer job after high school at a studio. He didn't have any background, he wasn't experienced. But, they could see that in his free time he was beginning to learn things. They hired him and now he's full-time. So, I feel that if you can get in there by offering to work for free, you're better off."

An internship will not only develop your skill set, but it also puts you in the right place when studios are looking to fill an unexpectant need.

"I think you have to position yourself for opportunities when they arise," advises Chris Ohlgren, master animator at Will Vinton Studios. "A studio will go through long dry spells without hiring anyone, and then a huge project will come in and they'll have to staff up rather quickly. Most of the time when that happens, the number of people they need are not available. And so during those rapid growth periods, people who don't have much experience almost always get hired. That's how I got in. So, if you're always sending your reel, and you continually keep in contact with the studio, you've got a good chance of getting in the door. The key is to be persistence."

"We do a lot of training," adds Digital Muse's John Gross. "We have an intern program where we've gotten a couple of our artists, so we do training when we can. But, often times what happens is a project comes in the door and we've got to get started on it pretty quick. Then, we don't have time to train people. We need to bring in people that are local, that live in town and know the software. So, if it's a project where we need to bring people in for four weeks, we'll look for someone local."

Making it happen

Finding yourself in Hollywood - if that's your dream - is not an impossible task. People tend to create their own barriers to success, and mental roadblocks lead the list.

"One of the things I ask all my students is, 'If you had a magic wand, what would you wish for?' says animation instructor and LightWave aficionado, Brad Carvey. "Surprisingly, to me anyway, only one in twenty is interested in going to Hollywood and working at a place like Station X. All the rest are looking at other alternatives because they don't want to be in L.A. I guess part of the perception is that working on film is beyond anything that they can do. I think it's hard for them to imagine the transition from being at a junior community college in Albuquerque, to working on *Titanic* for Digital Domain. I think they're a little intimidated by Los Angeles."

Yet, the ranks of today's studios are staffed with people who did just that, says Scottish-born supervising animator John Allardice.

"Getting into the effects business in Hollywood is an accomplishable task," proclaims Allardice. "*You can do it*. That's what you've got to remember. Never think, 'No, that's too far fetched. I'll never get into it.' Everyone that's got into it was just an ordinary bloke who actually got their reel out the door and sent it to somebody. There was nothing particularly *special* about these individuals. They just worked hard at something they enjoyed."

What does it take to be successful?

There are plenty of attributes that make up a successful career. Those in the field know that the key ingredient is a very strong desire to make things happen.

"It definitely takes extra effort," says Rhythm & Hues' Pauline Ts'o. "You shouldn't go into this profession unless you have a *passion* for it, because it's a lot of hours. Sometimes you have to make sacrifices.

For instance, when I was in college, I made the very conscious decision to give up music. I took piano lessons for ten years and knew I was never going to be a professional musician. I knew that I was going into this technical program and I wanted to keep my visual arts up, and that was going to take time. So, something had to give. For some people, it might mean giving up something like that, or it might mean giving up surfing, or whatever. But in college, students really need to learn *how* to learn and never stop. I'm still taking art classes now. College can only prepare you to get your foot in the door. From there you will continue to learn and grow. You have to because this industry changes so quickly. The software that you learn one year is going to be completely different in three years. So, if you just learn what button to push and you don't understand *why* you're pushing that button, it's going to be really difficult."

"You can survive if you approach it with a job mentality," says John Allardice of Foundation Imaging, "but I don't think you'll excel. That's because there just so much work to put into this job to make something absolutely perfect. You've got to have a feel for it. You have to have a *love* for it to be able to bring the shot up to the level that is needed. Yea, you can do a perfectly adequate shot if you know where the buttons are and what to push, but you can't do a money shot that way, you can't get something inspired. You really have to have something within you that *wants* to do this stuff and *will not* let it out of your hands until it's absolutely perfect."

"I think students really need to focus on dedication and practice," advises Digital Muse executive producer John Gross. "Those are the things that got me where I'm at today. I would go home from work and play on the computer all night long. I literally did that all the time until I knew that software in and out. And then, I was persistent about getting out there and trying to get in someplace. I got lucky because I fell into a place that needed somebody right away. But its just a matter of pounding the pavement. Getting your demo reel out there and showing people what you can do. If you want to be good, you've got to put in the time. It's not a nine to five job."

"If you're thinking about getting into the high-end film business, you'd better love film," says Station X's Grant Boucher. "You'd better *love* what you're doing. The difference between the people who make it out here and those that don't is that the successful people love doing visual effects and they love films. You have to have a *passion* for it.

A lot of people decide they like this, but not enough to make a career out of it. They'd rather make it a hobby. Then, there are some people that just burn up with excitement. They're at the greatest risk of becoming frustrated trying to get into the business. They shouldn't. If you get out here in less than three years - from the time you first start until the time you get your first professional gig - count yourself very, very fortunate."

"Make sure you really *love* the business of film and animation," says twenty-five year visual effects expert John Follmer of Metrolight Studios. "Don't get into it just because it's hot right now. I know a lot of people who are really excited about getting into the business, and they aren't even sure what it is. Over a long term career, you realize, it's not easy. There are a lot of tough times. And there are a lot of times when nobody cares about the business. Right now, it's really hot. Everybody's interested. I think there will be a time when that will cool down. You should just be excited about doing the day to day work. Not because it's a cool field, but because you *love* it. There are long hours - ten hours a day is an average, but there's months you'll work straight through. I think it's more demanding than most jobs. It definitely takes more of your life. You just really need to *love* what you do."

"I've had a couple of friends that I've sat down in front of LightWave," says Bruce Branit, creative director at Digital Muse. "I've shown them a demo and a few things that I've done. And immediately, there is one of two responses: 'Wow, that's kind of neat!' or 'Move aside. I want to sit down and play with this.' We've had the same kind of response from our interns. Some come in and do their work and go home. Others are here twenty-four hours a day learning the software. If someone *loves* doing this, sooner or later they're going to get paid for it. I think some people find out there is pretty good money to be made in this field and so they get into it for that reason. Those people are never the best artists, because they're drawn to it for the wrong reason."

"Here's the illustration I use for success," says veteran freelance animation director Joe Conti. "My roommate from college came out to L.A. wanting to break into the business. Fred had a film degree like I did, but he never pursued it. Instead, he became a manager at Blockbuster Video in New Jersey. Seeing my career grow and change, he got excited enough to come out and visit me. And he said, 'What do I do? Where do I go? How can I make this happen?' I said, 'You're going to need to make an investment. You're going to need to get a computer, a copy of LightWave, and you're going to need to spend the next three months eating, sleeping, and drinking the software.' So, Fred didn't go get a job. He went into debt, charging everything on his Visa card. I'm sure he went tens of thousands of dollars into debt in order to learn LightWave on a crash course. After three months of busting his butt, he said, 'Okay, I'm ready. Give me a test.' I said, 'I want you to model the Titanic.' I gave him pictures of it and I said, 'Here you go. Model it and if you make it look good - you're hired. If it looks like crap, forget it. You'll need to go find another job somewhere else.' Now, Fred had no other job. So, he was *highly* motivated. (laughs) He went home, he built this thing, and he came back to me and he showed me some stills. I said, 'You're hired. Consider it done.' The irony is that Fred went on to build the digital model for the motion picture, *Titanic*.

"That's a success story. Now, for every success story there are ten failures. That's because people *don't* want to put in the time. They *don't* want to put in the energy. They *don't* want to put in the sacrifice. The people I hired for *Seaquest* didn't do it for money. They were hobbyists, and did it for nothing. They learned LightWave because they were *passionate* about it. That's the bottom line that will separate the people that will be successful from those that won't.

"I had a friend in television recently who wanted to learn a new job," Conti recalls. "I lent him a computer and all the software. Soon he was moaning, 'It's too hard.' He wanted to go out and chase women and go drinking. Later, there were about fifty openings for artists. He could have moved right out there and gotten a job if he had learned it. But the reality was he just wasn't passionate about it. Even though I *gave* him everything, it didn't solve the problem.

"What it really comes down to is you need to spend a couple of hours a day in front of a computer screen learning 3D animation. And if you don't want to do it, you shouldn't bother. Because you're never going to be happy. Unfortunately, a lot of people look at me and they see my success - a nice car, an airplane, and a nice home - and they say, 'Joe has it easy.' They have no idea how hard it has been. For the longest time I did it, and there was no money. The only thing that has carried me through is my *passion* for doing it. When I talk to students, I tell them, 'You have to *love* doing it. If you don't love doing 3D animation, then don't pursue it. Because you'll never be good at it.' And that's really true about any career you get into. Don't ever choose a career path just for the money. Because in any business, *money is just a gauge of how much you love doing what you do.*"

Without a doubt, success boils down to one word - *passion.* Long hours, impossible deadlines, and incredible challenges will quickly take their toll on even the most vivacious spirit. Only one trait seems to be able to overcome the difficulties that inevitably slip into any career path - *passion.* You've got to have it, if you expect to survive in this business.

Building a career

Having that special hunger is just the beginning, as anyone who has been in the business for any length of time will tell you. It's going to take time to absorb it all. And it's going to take a lot of work on your part.

You're not going to be a star right away. You should go into your first job and look for the person who has the most experience - the top dog - at that facility and try to get that person to be your mentor. Gravitate toward those who can help you develop your skills. Look at your first job as a continuation of your education. Learn the value of *all* of the tools at your disposal. That's the sign of a true craftsman.

Look at what a good wood worker uses. He uses a multitude of sanders - a belt sander, an orbital sander, a palm sander, and a corner sander. That's what you have to realize as an animator. Everything has a purpose. Be willing to use whatever is out there.

Help sell your team

Just as there are many tools to complete a job, it takes many players to make a studio team complete. Support your team by being the best you can be in all areas.

Learn to ignore the lines that seem to be drawn by titles. Becoming an accomplished animator doesn't mean that you don't have to know anything about modeling. Being a superb technical director doesn't mean that you shouldn't learn what it takes to create a terrific character performance. The most successful players learn as much as they can about *all* aspects of their profession.

There is one role that is often overlooked by team players, and one that you can easily take on with little additional effort. It's a role that's key to your survival.

"I use to think that when you worked at a facility, you just did your job," says Grace & Wild Studios graphics coordinator Carl Scott. "But that's not true. When you work at a studio, not only do you do the work, you *sell* too. You have to be bringing in clients or you'll find your financial safety net will disappear in a hurry. This is not a welfare job. If you're not busy, you'd better find out why.

"You can help sell a facility three ways. One, being friendly - just smile. Two, being knowledgeable - know what you're doing. Three, do whatever it takes to meet a deadline. Learn to show an interest in the clients that come into the facility. A simple, "How's it going?" when you see a client in the hallway makes a world of difference. Selling a facility is less about banging on doors and more about representing the facility you work for in a favorable light. You want your clients to see you as a friendly person who's fun to work with. That's what gets clients to come back to you. It's not about the expensive equipment that surrounds you. Every studio has the same toys. The difference is the attitude of the people that operate the machinery."

Reaching the top

There's an old story that a successful person is like a three legged stool. They stand on talent, speed, and personality. If any one of those traits is lacking - no matter how strong the other two - you'll never be successful.

You can be incredibly talented and a have a great personality, but if your work is slow - you'll never finish in time. If you have amazing speed and a great personality, but have no talent - you won't produce anything worthwhile. And if you're the fastest, most talented person ever, but you can't get along with people - no one will ever work with you. If you're strong in all three areas, *no one can stop you*.

Talented people will always be a rare commodity. Finding a talented individual who possesses an aggressive work ethic, a responsible mentality, and a *passion* for what they do is rarer still. If you're that kind of person, you'll find an animation industry waiting with open arms.

Chapter 5:
Working Freelance

For many, the freedom freelance work provides is more appealing than working for someone else. You can set your own hours, pick and choose the clients you prefer, and potentially generate more income than you can working for a studio. These are just a few of the luring qualities that attract people to the freelance market every year. Of course, there are plenty of pitfalls. Having worked in the freelance arena for ten years, I can honestly say, I wouldn't trade the lifestyle for anything. But, honing the business skills necessary to maintain a successful freelance operation requires time, patience, and a good deal of common sense. In the next few pages, I'll impart what it takes to achieve success as a freelance animator.

Ignorant bliss

I was a successful radio announcer and video producer when first introduced to the idea of freelance computer animation. I had always been interested in animation ever since I was a kid. Flipbooks, home made Zoetrope wheels, and 8mm animated films were all part of my childhood. The idea of getting back into animation as an adult caught my fancy when I started reading about desktop animation in the mid-1980's. I was familiar with professional animation tools like Symbolics, which I had encountered while producing for CBS/Fox Video. At that time, professional systems were large, cumbersome, expensive boxes that generally created nothing more than splashy flying logos. They cost upwards of $150,000 dollars and took several days to render a few seconds of material. The idea that these machines could one day churn out character animation was unheard of - and really quite impossible given the technology.

One day, I was in need of chucking my typewriter for a word processor. I learned of a computer called an Amiga which had some pretty terrific video graphic capabilities - far superior to anything else on the desktop market. I sold my record collection and bought a used one, figuring I could write video scripts and dabble with computer graphics. I started reading whatever I could about Amiga-based software, and eventually bought a 3D animation program called Sculpt 4D. The manual was thick, not terribly clear, and the interface difficult to navigate. But, over the course of several weeknights, I managed to figure out how to create a cube, light, and animate it. It took sixteen hours to render one frame, and over a week to generate a half second! You have to realize how exciting it was to create something at home on a desktop computer, that required nearly a quarter million dollar system only a few years earlier. It didn't take a genius to see the writing on the wall. I could feel my dreams of creating animated films being revived.

The notion really took off when I picked up a copy of *Amiga* Magazine's Animation Special in January 1989. The annual issue charted the latest hardware and software achievements as well as people around the country who had found success as desktop computer animators. On one page, I spotted a profile about "Larry," who had started up a desktop business in California creating video productions which included his own computer generated flying logos. There was a picture that showed Larry seated next to a stack of video decks, in front of his computer monitor. I immediately thought, "If he can do it, I can do it." With visions of Larry's success in my head, I set off on a course that ultimately has brought me much success - and quite a few painful lessons. Ironically, I later met my inspiration at a trade show and found out that all was not what I had imagined. It turns out that Larry was involved in production for just a few months (during the time the article was written), later quit to get into software development, and at the time of our meeting wasn't doing computer animation at all! Had I known the truth of the situation, I might never have embarked down the road I'm on now. Thankfully, I didn't know any better. You'll find that sometimes, ignorance *is* bliss.

Getting your bearings

There's really no sense in reinventing the wheel, and since I've been down the road you're considering (along with quite a few others), I've got some suggestions that'll make your ride a lot smoother.

Working freelance can be a tough row to hoe. I had a wealth of video production experience to draw from, as well as contacts in the industry that helped get me started. You may not be as fortunate. That doesn't mean your task is impossible. You've just got more to learn before you can become effective.

One of the hardest issues to deal with is fear. This is the one emotion that will stop most people in their tracks. Besides being an accomplished animator, you're going to need to market your services, find clients, deal with cash flow issues, tackle paperwork, handle your own accounting, deal with computer maintenance problems, and many other issues. For most people, the prospect of facing all of these challenges is truly frightening. It certainly was for me. But what I found is that if you attack each problem as it occurs your workload becomes quite manageable. Remember, successful people do not lack fear, they *continue in spite of it*.

Persistence

The key ingredient to your success is persistence. Eighty-five percent of people give up before they reach their goal - many unaware that success is just around the corner. Whatever you do, *don't quit*. When you quick, you lose. As long as you persist, there is a chance of success. It's been my experience that just getting started puts you ahead of fifty percent of the population who only *wish* their dreams would come true. Persistence, and persistence alone, is the single greatest attribute of a successful person. More than knowledge, talent, or connections - persistence will enable you to realize your dreams.

Naysayers and advice

Be prepared to run into plenty of people who seem to thrive on the failure of others. The fact of the matter is most people haven't realized their dreams. And people don't want to be reminded of that fact. Your success will become a reminder to them. In order to avoid that, people will often dole out "advice" to help you in your career choices. Of course, most of the advice is nothing more than a reason *why* they think you're going to fail. You'll get advice like this from family, friends, and other people you respect and admire. That's what makes it terribly confusing. They *do* have your best interests at heart, don't they? Not always.

One of the classic freelance success stories is that of Joe Conti. A pioneer in desktop computer animation, Conti has accumulated an impressive list of credits over a ten year period including: *Unsolved Mysteries, Star Trek: The Next Generation, Viper, Hercules: The*

Legendary Journeys, Michael Jackson's *History* music video, *Courage Under Fire, Men in Black,* and *The Siege* - to name just a few. Had Conti listened to "advice" from friends and co-workers, he might never have done any of it.

"I started off as an engineer, then switched majors and went to film school," explains Conti. "And everyone said, 'You'll never get a job.' So, when I graduated I felt like I was lost and nobody was going to hire me, so I enlisted in the military for two years. That was the best experience of my life. They taught me self confidence and reminded me that I'm not going to live forever. I learned that you really have to go after the things that are most important to you - to *pursue your dreams* no matter what, because someday it's all going to be over and you're going to have missed out. So, when I got out, I stopped listening to the naysayers.

"I've been hearing, 'You can't do it,' my whole career. When I worked at Apogee, everyone laughed and thought it was totally ridiculous that I was going to use an Amiga computer and LightWave to do visual effects. At the time, Apogee was working with PDI and all these high-end companies that had millions of dollars in SGI's. Of course, millions of dollars in SGI's back then is the equivalent of a couple of DEC Alpha's today. So, they laughed at it. A television production company called up and they wanted some effects, and Apogee just laughed at them because they had $40,000 dollars, and Apogee only did $10 to 20 million dollar effects budgets. But, I convinced the president to give me a shot with my Amiga, and it happened to be the opening season of *Unsolved Mysteries.* It became the number one show for the week - 60 million viewers - and they were so blown away by the effects that news companies were calling us up and asking, 'How did you do it?' And nobody believed we did it on the Amiga using LightWave. I left Apogee, set up shop in my apartment in California, and started doing episodes of *Unsolved Mysteries* out of the apartment. All of a sudden, this $40,000 per episode - that was usually going to this big company - was going directly into my pocket. So, suddenly the low guy on the production totem pole was making far more money than any individual artist at any high-end visual effects company in L.A. But, nobody wanted to believe it.

"That's been a theme my whole life. When I first moved to L.A. everyone said, 'It's impossible, you'll never make it, it's too difficult, give it up.' When I left L.A. and moved to New Mexico, everyone said *exactly* the same thing. So my whole life has been, 'You can't do it on

LightWave, it's impossible. Don't pursue your dreams, you'll never make it.' The week I moved to Albuquerque, I landed the largest music video ever produced - Michael Jackson's *History* - which had a budget of $4 million dollars. So the irony is that within one week of leaving, I made more money than in the seven years that I lived in Los Angeles. I was working out of the dining room of my house on all these projects. I had rendering machines in the garage, rendering machines in bedrooms, cables spewing out everywhere - I was doing $1 million dollars-plus work and it was all done using Amiga 2000's, Screamer net and the Raptor MIPs rendering boxes.

"I went to NAB (National Association of Broadcasters) in 1995 as a guest speaker, and I was telling everybody how we were doing the work in LightWave. I had people get up to my face and tell me it was *impossible*. These were hard core high-end 3D people, and they got up and they said straight out, 'It's bullshit that you're doing this stuff at your house on an Amiga. It's impossible.' No matter.

"In 1996, I started getting calls for big feature films. The first one was *Courage Under Fire*. That led to *Men in Black*, and the opening dragonfly sequence in 1997. For the rendering, we gutted one of my closets, and stacked it full of rendering boxes. We did that because it was quiet and we could air-condition the closet. The movie was a big success, and everyone saw the opening two minute sequence. But again, the same comments followed, 'LightWave couldn't have done it. No way. It looked too good.' In fact, it looked so good, that ILM - who did all the other effects - is often credited for the opening sequence.

"Now, I'm producing my own film projects, and picking and choosing other feature and commercial work that looks interesting. The actual amount of time I work is probably three to four months out of the year. And I make a year's salary. I left L.A. because I decided I really wanted my life to be great *all* the time - I wanted to fly my plane, I wanted to ride dirt bikes in the desert, and I wanted to take trips. Now, I make enough money to support that lifestyle, and I've been really successful at maintaining that.

"Guess what? Now I've got people saying, 'I had it easy.' (laughs) Nobody knows how hard it was for all of us starting out with LightWave and trying to prove to the industry that it was possible. *Nobody* knows how hard it was.

"The message here is that you *have* to pursue your dreams. You just *have* to push forward and do what you believe in. Everyone has constantly given me the wrong advice. *Constantly*. Even people in the business. You have to understand that when you leave to pursue your dreams, it sort of makes people who don't pursue their dreams hope that you fail. Because if you succeed, it makes them feel bad.

"When I went to L.A., all the people that were advising me not to go were people who hadn't followed *their* dreams. I could see that the thought of me making it in Los Angeles would force them to look back at their own lives and say, 'What did I do? Where am I?' When I left L.A. it was the same thing, because in some ways the people who are there, *don't* want to be there. They don't want to be in Los Angeles. They want to be somewhere else, but they don't have the ability to leave. So, when they hear me saying, 'I'm going off to New Mexico to ride dirt bikes and work on films,' that's a horrible thought to them. Because it forces them to examine their own lives and wonder, 'What about me?'

"I've constantly pursued what I believe is most important to *me* my whole life, and somehow that formula has worked really well. I could have stayed in Los Angeles and worked on *Titanic* for Digital Domain. Of course, when I saw *Titanic*, I wish I had worked on it. But, at what price? To give up pursuing my own dreams? For me, being on my own, doing what I want to do, when I want to do it, spending time with the ones I love, and pursuing my dreams, is what it's all about."

Pursuing your dreams is not an easy road. One of the major stumbling blocks is *bad* advice. Whenever someone offers you advice, ask yourself, "Is the person offering advice where I want to be?" If not, ignore it. If true, weigh the advice with your own experience and act accordingly.

Chapter 6:
Setting Up Shop

Let's get down to the business of establishing yourself as a freelance computer animator. There are several business decisions you'll have to make, so let's get them out of the way. Keep in mind that sound legal advice should always be sought out when establishing a business. This book can only present what I encountered in the state of Michigan as an entrepreneur. Laws are different in each state, and only an attorney familiar with the laws of your state should be sought for advice. Although there are some things you can do on your own, the following pages are not meant to serve as a substitute for legal advice.

Naming Your Business

First, you need to decide on a name for your business. You may want to do business under an assumed name or your own. There are pros and cons to choosing a business name, so here's a few tips:

"Doing Business As" (DBA) - This gives you a company name and allows you to operate legally. It's not that you couldn't just make up a name, print up stationary, and hang a sign on your house (ordinances permitting). You could. But, if someone using the name legally objected, you'd find yourself changing your business name at a considerable expense. You might as well do it right the first time. You'll find it's not hard at all. You could do business as, "John Smith Productions," "Digital CyberPunks," or anything else you dream up. The choice is yours. The only requirement is that no one else can be doing business in the county you live in using the same name. The best thing to do is to come up with three good choices. Then, go down to the county seat and register the name with the county you live in. This is required by law. If there is a conflict with someone already registered, they'll tell you. Simply use the next name on your list. Business names which include your name are pretty safe bets, unless you have a very common name.

Before you invest countless hours dreaming up a business name, here are some things to consider:

(a) **Avoid cute names.** Your business name should identify the business you're in. If you have to explain it, it doesn't work. "Digital CyberPunks" doesn't define the business. Is it an internet company? Is it a rock band? Don't make people guess.

(b) **Avoid all encompassing words.** Remember, you're trying to define your business. For example, avoid words like: digital (everything's digital today), and cyber (nearly a cliché). Use words like "animation," "studios," and "productions," to help shape your business image.

(c) **Avoid words that conjure negative images.** "Satanic Animation Weirdo's" probably won't get you any work from the more conservative corporations. On the other hand, "Wood Creek Animations," invokes soothing images.

(d) **Avoid home-office names.** Words like: "Associates," and "Enterprises" are typical home-office fare. These are red flags that signal you're working out of your home (you are, but you don't want people to think that).

Your company name should sound impressive. Short names are easier for clients to remember. Flip through the Yellow Pages to get ideas. Get creative!

Incorporating

Incorporating your business is easier than you think, and provides tax advantages as well as some basic protection from lawsuits. An attorney or tax accountant can advise you about your options and explain your rights. Most will want to charge you $200-500 dollars to fill out the articles of incorporation (a two page form), but you can do it yourself. It's quite easy.

If you incorporate, you don't need to register a DBA with the county seat. Your business name will be filed at the state level as a corporation. The same rules apply - you can't use a business name already on file. If you plan to incorporate, you can telephone your state's Department of Commerce - Corporation and Securities Bureau and have them check the availability of the business name you've selected. While you have them on the phone, request a copy of their Articles of Incorporation. This is the form you'll fill out to establish your corporation.

Once you find your business name is available, you can move forward. Fill out the Articles of Incorporation and return them with the filing fee (usually around $20.00).

Establishing yourself as an S-corporation is best when you're starting out. Talk to a tax accountant to understand the benefits.

Employer Identification Number (EIN)

You'll also need to obtain an Employer Identification Number (EIN) from the Internal Revenue Service. This number is used to identify your business account, and related tax returns and documents, even if you do not have employees. Ask for form SS-4, Application for Employer Identification Number. Keep the number assigned to you handy. You'll need it for a number a business related transactions.

Bank Accounts

Once your Articles of Incorporation are processed and returned, you can go to the bank and open a business account. Take the Articles with you, the bank will want to keep a copy on file. When selecting a check book, ask for the type that provides carbonless copies. When you write a check, you're provided a copy which can be stapled to the invoice and forgotten until tax time. You'll find this feature more than handy. For size, a pocket check book may be more practical than the big binder style.

Insurance

Contact your insurance agent and make sure you get your computer equipment insured. Whether you're a homeowner or a renter, you can get insurance to protect you from fire and theft. Don't assume your homeowners insurance covers you! Protect your investment! The insurance company will need a list of all of your equipment, serial numbers, and value. Insure your equipment (hardware & software) for the replacement value. When your policy comes up for its annual renewal, you can drop items that have little or no value.

Logos

Create a logo for your company. Design something that works well for stationary. You can use a program like Illustrator to do your own, or hire someone to design one for you.

Stationary

This is the most important part of establishing your business image. What your business cards, letterhead, and envelopes look like will speak volumes about your business. Don't skimp on paper quality. You want your letters and cards to stand out. Use a textured linen paper. Look into raised inks, embossing, and foils to accent your logo. Dies, paper, inking and quality printing will cost you $500-700 dollars. Remember, your stationary is your building. Give it a solid, established feeling with classy stationary.

Get Listed

Forget the yellow pages. Production people don't look for services there. They use specialize production guides. Most states have at least two production guides you'll want to get listed in. These production guides are published once a year (usually in the first quarter) and contain listings for all production houses, producers, animation studios, freelancers, and service people. The guide is a "yellow pages" of production services and is used throughout the year by producers of programming. The exposure is good, and inexpensive to get listed - usually less than $50 dollars (and in some cases, free!). At the state level, contact your Office of Film and Television (or similar entity), and ask if they produce a production guide. Most large cities also have a producers association which publishes a guide. Finally, check with an advertising guild or association who may distribute a similar publication.

Advertising

When most people start a business, the first thing they think about is advertising. Although this sounds like a good idea, it's an expensive proposition for a start-up home business. A black and white quarter page ad can cost several hundred dollars to produce and as much as $500 dollars to place (per issue!). A color ad of equal size can triple those numbers. Most people don't have the kind of marketing budget to sustain that level of advertising, especially when you consider that you'll need to run your ad several times over a six month period to see any tangible results.

A less expensive approach to take is direct mail. Today's offset printers can produce a full color postcard (with a black & white message on the reverse side) for a fraction of the cost of a black and white magazine ad. You can have 1,000 postcards like this printed up for less than $250 dollars. If you design the card yourself, using Adobe Pagemaker (or a similar page layout program), you can eliminate your out-of-pocket production costs. The only other expense is postage!

The most effective direct marketing is targeted to your specific audience. Create a mailing list from one of the production guides in your area. Include producers, advertising agencies, and post-production houses. Direct marketers know that a targeted list will generate sales of at least 1.5% percent. So, you'll need a sizable mail list to insure call backs that result in sales. You'll also need to do repeated mailings - to keep your name in front of the client. Send a batch of postcards out, wait thirty days, and repeat the process.

For better results, vary the image and message on the postcard. Print three variations of the postcard and rotate the mailings. For the price of a single full color magazine ad, you could run a one year direct advertising campaign!

Trade magazines

Once you start getting work, send press releases and screen shots to all the major trade magazines. The placements are free, and the publicity will get you noticed.

"When we finished our first character animated commercial we sent a screen shot into all the trade magazines," says Jeff Barnes, executive producer and co-founder of Computer Cafe. "*Post* magazine published the screen shot and we got a call from the executive producer of Pillsbury Dough Boy at PDI, asking, 'Who are you guys? What is this?' The animation was very rough, but the screen shot looked great. (laughs) That's when we realized the power of PR and marketing. In fact, that's how we built the company. Every time we finished a job, we'd flood the market with screen shots, and write a little press release. Not that you'd ever get any work from that, but you get your name out there. You get kind of legitimized that way."

Not all trade magazines will run your press clippings every time, but a few dollars in stamps more than pays for itself in publicity when they do.

Chapter 7:
Your Payment Policy

Cash flow is the life-blood of your business. To stay in business and out of the financial frying pan you need to establish a payment policy and stick to it.

How to Charge

Before you get that first animation project, you'd better figure out how you're going to charge the client for your services. There are a variety of ways to structure your rate. Here are the most popular pay scales to consider:

(1.) **Hourly.** This is the most familiar way to bill. It's comfortable because it's the way most people get paid in the "real" world. However, the hourly pay structure is *not* in your best interests as a creative person. Let's face it, being creative is not a nine-to-five job. You may get a brainstorm at 9:00 p.m., slide into your home office, and work until midnight experimenting with a new approach. How do you bill those hours? Straight time? Overtime? Trying to figure it all out can make you dizzy. It is also difficult to apply a single hourly rate considering the many roles you'll play as a freelance animator. Through the course of a typical project you'll serve as consultant, storyboard artist, producer, graphic artist, animator, technical engineer, telephone receptionist, and administrator. Typically, each role would be on a different pay rate. How do you calculate when your role as producer ends, and your job as animator begins? Using an average pay figure for the combined roles will find you being underpaid *most* of the time. Finally, it is difficult - if not impossible - for a client to get involved with a vendor without knowing *exactly* what the project will cost. The client doesn't want to get an unexpected bill at the end of the project because you had to work more hours than you (or they) figured. It's nearly impossible to predict how many hours a project will require before you start. The best you can do is provide an educated guess. An hourly pay structure under these circumstances is a blueprint for disaster.

Someone is going to take a financial bath, and that person is likely to be *you*! If you pass the buck to the client, *you* lose again - killing any repeat business by destroying the good will and trust you've worked hard to build.

(2.) **Weekly.** This is the equivalent of a salary, and contains as many pitfalls as an hourly rate. Predicting how many hours you'll put into a project in a given week is all but impossible. Projects that require multiple weeks inevitably draw more hours as the project reaches maturation. Those final weeks will find you working for a fraction of what you were being paid during the startup. Because of the custom nature of each project, you'll find it difficult to settle on a weekly pay rate that will work in all situations.

(3.) **Per Project.** This is the best way to structure your rate. It provides control and incentives for both client and freelancer that is hard to match in any other rate structure. For the client, the structure is ideal. They know *exactly* what the job will cost before making a commitment. Once a deal is struck, the client understands that any changes in the project will result in additional charges that will be negotiated at the time of the change. This encourages clients to stick to the project plan, since modifications carry with them the burden of additional costs. The per project rate structure is equally favorable for you, the freelancer. You know exactly how much you will be paid for a given project. You'll never have to worry about working for "free" because a client changed the parameters midway through the project. The trick to making a per project bid work is your ability to accurately estimate what it will take in time and materials to deliver the project. The client feels comfortable with this arrangement because any mistake in your estimate is absorbed by you. Both parties get what they want. The client gets a firm price with no surprises, and you get financial control over your time.

What's Not Negotiable

There are many things that are negotiable in a business relationship. However, the terms under which you will be paid should *never* be used as a bargaining chip. Consider these elements to be non-negotiable. There are plenty of reasons to be flexible with your creative ideas, your schedule, and how you can best serve your client. However, being paid in a timely fashion is one area you *need* to have the final word on.

I had a client who wanted a $2,000 dollar flying logo done for his company. I met him at his company offices in Windsor, Canada - across the river from my hometown of Detroit, Michigan. Both the client and his offices were impressive, which put me at ease. When it came to the terms of the agreement, he explained that he couldn't put any money down on the project, but would pay in full on delivery. Against my better judgment, I agreed. It took a week to create the ten-second logo. When it was time to deliver I called and asked him to stop by my studio to pick it up. He told me his schedule wouldn't allow it and asked if I could come to Canada and meet him at his office. I agreed and drove to his office. When I handed him the master tape, he told me the check wasn't ready but he would bring it by my office the next day. I bit, and left without being paid. Guess what? I never saw him again. A short time later, I was contacted by a private detective who informed me that my client was an ex-con who had skipped town after scamming a number of people (myself included). Apparently, the logo I had created was used to con investors into participating in a non-existent television show. It turned out that the client was wanted in the U.S. for a parole violation related to a previous forgery conviction. That explained why all of our business was conducted in Canada. This entire sorry episode could have been avoided had I insisted on sticking to my payment terms.

Remember, *never allow a client to dictate the terms of how and when you will be paid*. The only way you'll stay in business is to control your own cash flow. And no one knows how to do that better than *you*, right? The quickest way to get into financial trouble is to allow a client to control your cash flow.

It's okay to offer a *choice* of payment plans to make it easier on the client, but the choices should be of your own making. Three variations come to mind immediately:

(1.) **Cash in advance.** This might work for smaller jobs (under $500), or when a client has an unreliable track record when it comes to paying on time.

(2.) **Half in advance, balance on delivery.** This is the most common form of payment. Make sure that 50% covers your costs or close to it. Think in terms of, if you only get that payment you're okay. That's how you price things in this range. If the client is unable to pay half up front, offer them the one-third payment plan. See below.

(3.) **One third in advance, one third at a specified mid-point, balance on delivery.** This works well for projects with long schedules. It also enables clients with little operating cash to get the project started, and pay as you go along. This is also ideal for you, because you'll have two-thirds of the payment before the project is complete. Again, make sure that the payment schedule covers your costs - in advance - as they are needed.

All three of these payment plans share one thing in common - you are *paid in full* before delivering the final product. Following this approach *without deviation* is the secret to maintaining good cash flow. In addition, it's good common sense.

You're not a bank

Think about it. There's not a place in America where you can buy goods or services without paying up front. Cars, homes, groceries, and cigarettes all require payment in advance, *before you take delivery*. Selling animation is no different. As a business person, you *must* collect your fee before turning over the merchandise. Once you give the client the finished animation, you have *nothing* to induce payment. Holding the completed animation until you're paid in full is the only way to keep from getting the short end of the financial stick.

I had a client once who leaned on our personal relationship to gain a thirty-day extension to the final payment of a three installment plan. I reasoned that with two-thirds of the money in my pocket, I could afford to grant them thirty-days on the final payment. What a mistake. The red flag went up when they failed to make the second installment. When called on it, they offered *half* of what they had agreed to in the contract. Eventually, I had to stop work (thereby jeopardizing their program deadline) in order to get the second installment. By then, the client had changed the terms of the contract by adding an additional minute of animation to the project, ballooning the final payment to an amount better than 50% of the entire project. When I informed them that I couldn't extend credit for that amount, the client became indignant and insisted they would hold me to the original thirty-day extension on the final payment. After a little detective work, I learned that the client owed money all over town (which explained the second installment fiasco), and was planning to stretch my generous credit extension indefinitely. I managed to get paid in full by taking the advise of my attorney and refusing to release the completed animation masters. In essence, I held the trump card which saved me from taking a very *big* financial bath.

Remember, *you're not a bank*. You don't give credit, and you don't extend payments. Hold fast to this rule of business and you'll never get stuck holding the bag.

As you make your way in the freelance world, you'll run into some people who don't believe in this rule. They believe that you should extend them credit for thirty, sixty, or ninety days. They believe that you're so desperate you'll do anything - including changing your terms of payment - in order to work with them. They'll even try to convince you that nobody in the production business works the way you do. I've got just three words of advice: *Don't believe them.*

The fact of the matter is it's *your* animation business. If people want to work with *you*, they'll do exactly what *you* say. The only people who ask for credit are the ones who won't pay anyway - even after ninety days! You don't need them. In fact, you want to avoid them. Don't get suckered into thinking that you're the only one who insists on being paid when the job is finished. Remember, the only people who'll question your payment policies are the ones who won't honor them anyway. Who needs that?

Chapter 8:
Finding Clients

One of the first questions you'll be asked by friends and family is, "Where are you going to find clients?" The answer? Everywhere! But first, you'll start with people you know. This is the foundation of every entrepreneurial business. Most people don't realize that doctors, dentists, florists, lawyers, butchers, and all sorts of business people begin their practice with friends and relatives. Give them a few of your business cards (don't be stingy!) or pass out your color postcard. Let them all know what you're doing. Don't expect to sit back and wait for the calls, even if you are lucky enough to have a video producer in the family. Your friends and family are simply the first level of the most effective form of advertising - *word of mouth*.

Word of Mouth

What's the first thing you ask a friend when you need a brake job on your car? "Do you know a good mechanic?" How about dining out? "Do you know a good restaurant?" What about the latest entertainment? "Seen a good movie lately?" When it comes to advice on spending money, we rely on the people we know to navigate the world around us.

People are naturally suspicious of advertisements. They prefer an independent opinion about a product or service. Get people talking about your business and you will have created an unbeatable sales force! There is nothing in the world as priceless as a kind word said about you and your services. *Make it a point to cultivate people who endorse your work*.

When the opportunity presents itself, talk about what you do. People are fascinated by animation! It's a part of the entertainment business, and they'll see you as a mini-movie mogul. People want to feel important, and for many, rubbing shoulders with extraordinary people like you fills their need! They'll want to talk about you to their friends. This is your biggest asset. Use this fact to your advantage. *Tell your friends what you want your potential clients to know*. Rest assured, your friends will deliver the message for you.

Remember, it's not important who *you* personally know. It's all the people your friends know, and their friends know, and so on. Successful word of mouth advertising is akin to dropping a pebble in pond and letting the ripples spread out to reach shores you could never reach otherwise.

You'll find that 90% of your business will come through people who have learned of your work through word of mouth. Therefore, you need to make sure that the people you encounter are getting the message you want potential clients to know:

(1.) **Quality.** Let people know the quality of your work. You don't have to beat them over the head. Just show them your work! The vast majority of people in business *do not* deliver quality work. (How many times have you been unsatisfied by poor workmanship or services?) Some don't care, and many are incapable of delivering it. If you consistently deliver quality services, people will beat a path to your door.

(2.) **Custom work.** Emphasize that each of your animations is a custom job, geared toward your clients and their individual needs. People love to purchase hand-crafted, one-of-a-kind items. It makes them feel important. Old world craftsmanship will always be in demand. That's because we view technology as cold and analytical. As technology continues to dominate our lives, we feel a *need* to reconnect with those things that remind us of our human side. We seek out ways to feel warm and understood. Focusing on the personal aspects of your work will draw clients toward you. Although having the fastest microprocessor, the biggest monitor, and the coolest software is interesting, it won't excite your clients. Technology is constantly getting smaller and faster. Chances are your competition has already got technology that is faster than yours. Forget trying to out gun the competition with technology. I have yet to see an animation created by a machine. It's people that create animation magic. Technology is simply their tool. Your clients are interested in what *you* can do, not your machine. To land the biggest accounts and garner the best clients, *always put craftsmanship before technology*.

(3.) **Price.** Never talk about the cost of your animations with anyone other than your clients. First of all, it's nobody's business what you charge. Secondly, it's irrelevant what you charged on past accounts. Each job is a custom job, and therefore unique. Thirdly, people outside of the industry haven't got the slightest clue what kind of an investment in time and money you've put into your animation business. Anything you say about pricing is liable to be misinterpreted. If you tell them the last job you did was billed at $10,000 dollars, what might they think? You charge a third of *their* yearly salary? You're living high on the hog? You can afford to slip them a loan? People automatically weigh dollar amounts in terms of their own station in life. A millionaire wouldn't blink an eye at a $10,000 dollar figure. A minimum wage earner might see *you* as a millionaire. Either way, the figure you quote might be misinterpreted as "cheap" or "outrageous," depending on whose ears it falls on. You don't want a potential client making up his mind about your work based on this kind of hearsay. The best way to answer the question (and your friends *will* ask you) is with a nonspecific response. You might say, "All my prices are custom, based on a per project quote," or "I quote per project," or "My rates are compatible with the marketplace." Don't feel the need to provide any more information than that. You'll find that *real* friends won't push the issue. Remember, *never talk price with anyone but your clients*.

Although getting friends and family to spread the word about your animation business is a start, you'll have to explore other avenues if you expect to make a living. Remember, word-of-mouth advertising is like planting seeds. Expect plenty of time to elapse between the planting and the harvesting. In the meanwhile, you need to go on the offensive and get a few jobs under you belt. Gain a few clients, and your confidence will grow along with your demo reel. Now, before you get out there to face the business world, you need to learn to protect the most precious asset you have as an entrepreneur.

Protecting your ego

One of the hardest things to maintain as a freelance animator is your self-esteem. Besides putting your creative abilities on the line every day, you'll have to face being rejected by prospective clients. Most people can't handle the "no's" that come with running a business. But, if you hope to become successful you'll have to find a way to handle rejection with grace, and come back for more. It's really not that hard, if you know a few secrets to maintaining a healthy ego.

(1.) **Feed your mind.** Most people eat three meals a day, but fail to feed their minds. Get in the habit of reading positive, motivating books on a *daily* basis. Keep in mind, you're not the first person who's started a business. There are hundreds of souls who have walked the same path and learned what it takes to handle rejection, face important decisions, and start the day with a spring in their step. Here are some classics to get you started:

(a) *How to Win Friends and Influence People*
       by Dale Carnegie
(b) *Think and Grow Rich* by Napoleon Hill
(c) *See You at the Top* by Zig Ziglar

You'll find these books (and much more!) in the self-help section of your local bookstore. You'll find a whole new world of possibilities (and great ideas!) open to you by reading positive thinking books. Simply spend twenty minutes a day - ten minutes in the morning, and ten before you go to bed - strengthening your self-esteem. You'll be amazed at what you can do once you start feeding your mind.

(2.) **Avoid naysayers.** Keep out of the way of those doom-and-gloom friends and relatives for the first few critical weeks. (After that, you won't care what they think!) The sad truth is there are people in your life who *want* to see you fail. In some strange way it makes *them* feel more secure. Don't let them get you down. Build up some success, before allowing any contact with them. If you do run across them, they'll likely ask, "Are you busy?" What they are *really* asking is, "Are you working?" What they *mean* of course is "Are you successful? Are you failing?" Your answer should always be the same: "Yes. I'm *always* busy." Nothing else. Don't offer any other details. The fact of the matter is, you *are* always busy. You're either busy with a current job, or you're busy looking for the next job. Either way, you fill your day. Let the naysayers wonder what you mean.

(3.) **Qualify potential clients.** Avoid cold calling. This is probably the least efficient way to find clients, and is absolutely devastating to your ego. Your mission is to wade through as few "no's" as possible to get to a client who says, "Yes!" Although you could stumble across a client by calling everyone in the telephone directory, you're liable to give up after a few hundred "no's." Don't put yourself in situations where the "no's" are likely to outweigh the "yes's." Instead, *qualify* the names on your list of people to call. Ask yourself several basic questions: Are they in the film & video industry? Have they purchased animations before? Do they have a project now that requires animation? If you don't know the answer to these questions, find out. Ask someone who works for them. Nose around. Do a little detective work. You'll find the payoff (a "Yes!") will be well worth it.

Remember, your self-esteem gets you out of bed in the morning. To guarantee success, learn to guard and nurture your ego.

Creating a Prospect List

To create a qualified prospect list, you'll need to gather the names, addresses and phone numbers of people who might be interested in buying your animation services. Where do you find qualified prospects? The best single source guide is the one available through your state's Film & Video Office. The guide is used to promote the state's technical and creative services to the Hollywood film community. (Be sure and get a listing in this guide.) Get a copy of the guide and check out the various subheadings. There are three key places to concentrate your efforts in your search for clients:

(1.) **Advertising agencies.** This is your best source for developing animation business. Your initial contact should be with the Creative Director (CD) of broadcast services. The CD can introduce you to other agency producers. Most guide listings will name the CD. Positions change frequently at advertising agencies, so always check the listing over the telephone before mailing anything.

Advertising agencies mark the beginning of the creative process. Their clients (Coca-Cola, American Airlines, General Motors, etc.) hire them to create advertising for print, radio and television. The advertising campaigns are usually coordinated - hence, part of the reason for an agency to design the whole campaign. Approaching an agency makes your job easier. Now, you don't have to sell your services to dozens of large corporations. You simply offer your services as a vendor to an agency who *represents* dozens of large corporations. The idea of using animation to sell a product always occurs early in the discussion process. By the time the commercial (or "spot") is filmed, it's already too late. You need to get to the people dreaming up commercial concepts if you hope to sell your animation services.

Call the agency and arrange a meeting with the creative director. Many times, the CD will have a few members of his staff on hand for your meeting. Show your reel and find out what accounts they handle. Gear your pitch toward the clients most likely to use animation to sell their products. At the close of the meeting, get each person's business card. (The new people you meet can be added to your contact list.) Each person is a lead to finding out about upcoming projects. You need to know what is going on inside the agency to get the jump on the competition. Keep in touch with each person you meet - phone them once every four to six weeks. Develop relationships. Remember, *people prefer to work with people they know*.

(2.) **Producers.** This is your second best source for developing animation business. There are many freelance producers who are hired directly by clients to produce advertising and promotional material for them. There are also plenty of advertising agencies who hire freelance producers on a per project basis. Some producers have long standing relationships with agencies and clients. Producers have a gold mine of contacts throughout the business which can help get you established in the creative community. Producers are usually called upon to consult or take an active part in the early creative process. Making the producers in your area aware of your abilities increases the likelihood that animation concepts will be discussed and implemented. You want to be the name they associate with animation in your area.

Contact the producers in your area and arrange to show them your demo reel. Find out how many animation projects they've done in the last year to get an idea of the level of opportunity. Always keep in mind that a producer with few past animation projects does not necessarily mean few future prospects. Many times, the lack of past animation work only signifies the lack of a reliable source. You can fulfill that role! Get the producer's card, and follow up with a contact call every four to six weeks.

(3.) **Post production studios.** This is your third best source for generating animation work. Most post production studios (or "houses") have graphic resources. In the past they were limited to edit-suite style graphics - two dimensional flying logos and art. Today, most post production studios are capable of creating both 2D and 3D graphic work. Fortunately for you, the 3D capabilities of the in-house animation artist are limited by the ever increasing demands of all of the other graphic work that must be created. You'll also find that post-production studios inevitably have "overflow" work - animation work that needs to be created at a time when their in-house artist is already booked. Post production studios never want to turn away work. They would rather subcontract the job to a dependable vendor and keep the client coming back to them. Getting your foot in the door at a local post production studio as their reliable vendor can lead to a comfortable supplementary income.

Contact the studio's graphic coordinator (or the production coordinator) and arrange to show your reel. Most post production house artists have a pretty good handle on 3D flying logos (after all, that *is* their bread and butter). Although it's always great to have a couple of spectacular logos on your reel (they'll need a good backup artist now and then), make sure your reel emphasizes specialty animation skills that studio artists *don't* have time to perfect - character animation and special effects. Show the coordinator how you can increase his studio's capabilities with your talents. Let them know you are available at a moments notice. Exchange cards, and keep in touch once every four weeks.

One word of warning: *Never use your relationship with a post production house to steal clients.* This is a sure way to kill your business. Film & video production communities are small, and word travels fast. It's okay if a mutual client approaches you *directly* after the successful completion of a post production studio assignment. However, you should *never* solicit a client while working for a studio or immediately after completing services as a vendor to a studio.

Making Contact

Handling yourself well during your initial telephone contact is paramount to establishing a good relationship with creative people. As you telephone each prospect on your list, keep in mind this single concept: *Respect their time.* Important people have little time to waste. When you spend too much time on the telephone chit-chatting you're telegraphing three things:

(1.) **You're not very busy.** How else do you explain the time you have available for a lengthy call? Of course, when you're first starting out you're *not* very busy. But, you don't want your prospect to know that. *Learn to act busy.* Important people don't have time to spend on calls of this nature. If they're interested in your service, they'll arrange the meeting and move on. Unnecessary chit-chat ("How's it going?" "Terrific weather were having, eh?" "How about that football game last night?") only tells them you've got time to burn, which can only mean one thing:

(2.) **You're not important.** Everybody wants to associate with the best people - the greatest mechanic, the best repairman, the top salesman. People in demand are exciting to be around. They're always on the go, working toward a goal or solution. You can hear it in their voice, their attitude, and their manner. They make others feel important and secure in the knowledge that everything is under control. You want your prospects to see *you* as that person - a person in demand. If you had a couple of projects due in the next few days, you wouldn't have time to waste with unnecessary telephone banter, would you? Important people don't waste the time of other important people. When you do, not only do you telegraph that *you're* not important, but also that:

(3.) **You don't think your prospect is very important.** Why would you waste their valuable time if you thought otherwise? Respect your prospect. Show them how important you think they are by getting right to the point of your call. Save the chit-chat for your face-to-face meeting. Develop an urgency in your voice that lets your prospect know that you've got a limited amount of time to speak on the telephone.

Controlling the Call

As we discussed earlier, protecting your ego is critical to surviving the rejection that can come when selling your services. When you make your initial contact with potential prospects, it's important that you maintain your confidence level no matter what happens during the conversation. One way to do this is to keep control of the conversation. This can be accomplished with very little effort, and without the prospect knowing what you're doing. Your ability to steer the conversation where you want it to go will increase your confidence level, thereby increasing your ability to get positive results.

There is nothing magical about this concept. In fact, it's one of the oldest sales techniques in the world. The secret is simple: *Ask questions.* The person asking questions controls the conversation. Most people feel obligated to respond to questions put to them. Follow an answer with another question, and you'll find that you can steer the conversation wherever you want to go.

Telemarketers use similar techniques (although they often sound stilted and scripted). "What long distance phone service do you use?" Respond to that question and you'll receive another until the telemarketer is selling you the benefits of switching long distance carriers. The solution, of course, is to simply not answer the question. But, you'd be surprised how many people are unable to do that. The reason is simple. *When asked a question, people feel obligated to answer.* You can use this universal personality trait to your advantage.

What to Say

Call your first prospective client - creative director, producer, or graphic coordinator - and arrange a meeting to show them your demo reel. When they come to the telephone, get right to the point.

"Hi, I'm John Smith and I'm a freelance computer animator. I was hoping to stop by this week and show you my reel. Do you think you'd be available later this week for about ten minutes?"

Avoid posing questions that might evoke a rejection. Don't ask, "Can I stop by?" Instead make a statement, "I was hoping to stop by." Then, follow the statement with a question that invites a response favoring you, "Do you think you'd be available later this week for about ten minutes?" The question suggests that the meeting is set, and only the date and time need to be determined.

The prospect will either agree to the meeting or not. If the response is favorable, offer a choice of two dates, "I could do something Thursday or Friday?" The question suggests you've got a full schedule. If neither of the suggested dates will work, allow the prospect to pick a date, "What would work for you?" Don't say another word. If you find the prospect being evasive and difficult to pin down, give them a chance to walk away. Don't let people feel cornered. You can take the pressure off by giving the prospect an out, "How about if I call you in a couple of weeks and we'll go from there?" Those people who grab the chance to put off making a commitment do so by agreeing to a future contact. Either way, you win.

The best creative people are constantly busy. You may have to wait until a project is complete before getting an appointment. Cultivate patience. By giving the prospect time to respond to your request you show respect for their time, and convey your willingness to wait. *Never look desperate*. Busy people are never desperate for work. Look busy to be busy.

When you land an appointment, keep dialing. Your confidence level will jump a notch after you nail down that initial meeting. Telephone another prospect *immediately*. You'll find yourself speaking more confidently, with additional control. It will actually get *easier* to book additional appointments. If you get a rejection, keep dialing. They can't stop you now. Your goal should be to set up several appointments in a row. Don't stop telephoning until you've reached that objective.

The Meeting

Although you suggested a ten minute meeting, most appointments last at least a half hour. If you make a good impression, the meeting might last an hour. Whatever the case, don't linger. Get right down to business and let the prospect dictate how long the meeting lasts.

You should be able to give your prospect a quick overview of your background and skills, and show your demo reel within fifteen minutes. If the client is interested, he'll start asking questions. Answer their questions, but *always ask your own*. What kind of projects do you most often handle? Is there a need for character animation? Do you do effects for television? Show an interest in the facility and what they're doing. Ask questions that help you determine how you might fit into their productions. Then, use the opportunity to show the client how your work would help them achieve their goals.

Besides showing the client what you can do, you want to walk away from the meeting knowing:

(1.) **Overall animation needs.** How often does the client encounter animation projects? What kind of projects are they? Logos? Character animation? Knowing the answers to these questions will tell you how often you should touch base with the client.

(2.) **Upcoming projects.** Find out if the client has any animation projects in the works. Many times the client is waiting to hear whether they've been awarded a bid on an animation project. Keeping current on which clients are getting animation work will help you focus your efforts.

You want to also leave the client with the following information:

(1.) **Demo Reel.** Leave a copy of your demo reel with the prospect. They need to be able to demonstrate to *their* clients that they have the resources to pull off an animation project. Help them sell *you*! Of course, it's possible the prospect could use your reel to sell a client on animation, then use another source to accomplish the task, leaving you out of the loop. Although it can happen, it's a risk you'll have to take. If it does occur, it's likely you'll find out about it soon enough. (Remember, the creative community is a small group of people.) *Never allow the client to include your work on their demo reel.* Keep your work separate and well marked (Your logo and phone number should be at the head and tail of your reel.) You don't want to appear to be their employee or associated with them in a way that puts off other area prospects. Remember, you're a gun-for-hire. Your loyalty is to the client who has the work.

(2.) **Contact information.** Leave your business card or a handout that gives the prospect plenty of ways to find you: telephone, fax, address, and e-mail. If you've got a website, suggest frequent visits to keep up to date with your latest efforts.

(3.) **Future meetings.** Let the client know that you'll check in from time to time. This is usually welcome and takes the pressure off the prospect from having to worry about keeping in touch with you. Remember, make it *easy* for them to deal with you.

When you feel the conversation begin to wane, end the meeting. Don't wait for the client to ask you to leave, "Well thanks for coming." Instead, *you* should bring the meeting to a close, "Well, thanks for having me. I appreciate the chance to talk with you." You don't need to run out the door, but you should wrap up the goodbyes promptly. By being the one to bring the meeting to a close, you show respect for your client's time, while conveying that *you* also have a busy schedule.

Learn to Make Opportunities

Don't make the mistake of going home, kicking up your feet, and waiting for the phone to ring. It may be a month or more before you get a call from these demo meetings. In fact, you may not get a call at all.

Getting work as a freelance artist requires *hustle*. You need to get out and *make* it happen. Most people *wait* for opportunity. You've got to *learn to make opportunity*. I have yet to meet a successful person who's had opportunity fall out of the sky and into their lap. Becoming successful is not a passive life style. You've got to take action!

After a successful demo meeting with a prospect, you'll have a feeling of exhilaration and accomplishment. You'll feel like you can do anything. Learn to *harness* that positive emotion, and propel yourself to a higher level of success. You should see as many prospects as possible after a successful meeting.

If you don't already have appointments booked, head home and make a few telephone calls. Set up the next couple of meetings. Positive emotions are contagious. People can hear it in your voice. The people you meet will spot that gleam in your eye, the bounce in your step, and the confidence you can't help but exude. They will feel drawn to you. Consequently, your chances of landing an animation project will increase dramatically.

Successful people learn early on that starting a new business is like trying to move a huge boulder. Getting it rolling can be backbreaking work. But once it starts moving - and this is extremely important - *it is easier to keep it moving*. Whatever you do, don't let your efforts come to rest. Keep moving.

When you experience success, capitalize on it by reaching out for more. Use your invigorated emotions to influence those around you. Get out and make more contacts. Create a desire in people that compels them to want to work with you. Remember, people want to be around those that make them feel good. Create that desire and you'll always be in demand!

Chapter 9:
Projects

Landing and completing a project involves a few basic steps. Although every job is different, your approach remains the same. Each step along the way is designed to give you the maximum amount of control over the project parameters. After all, your mission is to earn a profit on the work you do. If you lose control of the project, you'll most assuredly lose time and money performing the work.

Gaining control of any project begins with your first contact with the client. You must exude confidence, and gain the client's trust. Once a client trusts your expertise, they'll gladly relinquish the leadership role to you. This is essential to bringing a project in on time and on budget.

Your first few client contacts will probably be awkward. That's okay. You can only gain the confidence you need through experience. Luckily, the experience necessary to succeed is not limited to your own. *Even the experience of others enables you to build your confidence.* The reason is simple.

Your lack of confidence stems from a fear of the unknown. You're not sure what to say, or how to say it. The knowledge that will help you to overcome your fear can come from many sources. Although you could eventually gain confidence through your own experience, you can create *instant confidence* by trusting in the experience of others who have already developed proven methods. Don't try to reinvent the wheel. Trust in the experience of others, and you'll save a tremendous amount of valuable time as you develop your business.

I developed the following guidelines over a ten year period of day-to-day business contacts. They will help you get up to speed quickly, and enable you to present a confident manner from the start.

Specifics of the Job

The first question you'll hear from a potential client is, "How much will it cost?" To answer that question, you've got to ask a few of your own. Your questions are designed to determine the parameters of the project. Until you qualify the project, you cannot estimate a cost. You need to find out the following information:

(1.) **Type.** Is the project a flying logo? Industrial animation? Character animation? Determining the type of animation will give you a good idea of the *difficulty* factor. Although creating an animated sequence is *never easy*, flying logos are generally less complex than industrial or character animations. Here are some of the considerations for each type of animation project:

(a) **Flying logos.** This usually involves designing a moving sequence based on a company emblem or logo. In most cases, you'll be given a business card or black & white stat of the company emblem. You'll need to scan the logo into your computer system and create a 3D model. This is the most time consuming part of the job. Most logos are trademarked and use specialty fonts that you'll have to create from scratch. The complexity of the logo will affect the modeling, surfacing. and animating phases of the project.

(b) **Industrial animations.** These are mechanical animations that illustrate machine operation or a manufacturing process. This kind of project is usually based on very specific instructions from engineers who have designed the machines or are involved in the manufacturing process. You'll need to meet with them to discuss your storyboards to make sure they are accurate. Even then, your animation will likely undergo a few alterations as the project proceeds. This is due to the difficulty that engineers have in communicating what the animation needs to show. No matter how good *you* are at taking notes, plan on a few revisions before the project is complete. Modeling these kind of projects can be extremely time consuming due to the need to adhere to exact specifications. In essence, you're being asked to reverse engineer an existing product or process. Although your client may supply you with an existing CAD model, there are innumerable problems associated with converting such a model to your animation system. Software programs designed to convert models between systems are marginally successful at creating ready-to-use models. You'll find plenty of time is absorbed eliminating duplicate points and flipping polygons before the model will be ready for use.

(c) **Character animations.** This is the most time consuming of all animation projects. Designing, modeling, and surfacing a character can take weeks to accomplish. Lip-sync character animation requires even more resources. There are ways to cut corners in order to save time and money, but most clients will expect Hollywood-style results in the end.

(2.) **Storyboards.** Does the client have an existing storyboard, or will you be creating the design? An existing storyboard can tell you a lot about the complexity of the project. If one is available, have the client fax you a copy. If you'll be designing the animation, figure in additional time to draw up a board and get it approved.

(3.) **Length.** How long will the final sequence run? Three seconds? Ten seconds? Sixty seconds? The total length of the animation will effect the amount of time it takes to setup, render, and transfer the sequence to a delivery medium. This is a key ingredient to determining cost.

(4.) **Schedule.** When does the client expect the project to be completed? Three days? Four weeks? The deadline will let you know whether you'll be working overtime to get the job done. A tight schedule may require you to bring in extra help to get the job done, increasing your costs. Although a leisurely schedule is preferred, it doesn't necessarily translate into decreased costs. Spacing a three day project over several weeks only ties up your time, and prevents you from excepting work that would actually pay for the time. Comparing the client's deadline with the time required to complete the project will let you know if additional charges are appropriate.

(5.) **Additional production.** Sometimes your client will require you to provide more than just animation services. They may need you to supervise the compositing of your animation elements with live background plates. Or, you may need to be on hand for a character voice recording session. In these situations, you'll be serving as producer and should bill the time accordingly.

(6.) **Delivery media.** What kind of medium does the client need the animation to be delivered on? Computer disc? Videotape? CD-ROM?

You may need to go to an outside source to get the images into a format your client can use. You'll want to build this cost into your quote.

Remember, you can never ask to many questions. The more you know about the specifics of the project, the better your chances of coming out of it with a profit. Asking questions is the key to revealing potential problems that will cost you. Watch for requests that seem small, but can eat up your time.

"Clients often slip something in that seems real easy," explains Michael Feder, producer at Blue Sky Studios. "For example, a client says, 'We have this little logo treatment. This thing flies on and we want you guys to come up with what it looks like.' Well that sounds real easy, but red flags come to mind with that kind of request. You can spend five or six weeks going back and forth designing a custom logo and a reveal. And that's not what the spot is all about. So, I always say, 'Why don't you give us the font design based on your art director, or if you like, we can design this logo based on our experience.' So, the detailing of what they're going to get is really important because a lot of times they ask for things that seem small, but it really throws off the schedule and the cost."

After qualifying the project parameters, tell the client you'll fax them a quote. *Never quote a price during this initial telephone call*. The best you can do is guess at the cost, and inevitably you'll miscalculate - high or low. You'll need to sit down and carefully go over the time and out of pocket costs the project is likely to incur. Only then will you be in a position to determine a fair price.

Getting multiple quotes is a standard way of doing business. Most clients won't expect you to quote them a price without taking time to consider the parameters. Simply thank them for the call, and tell them you'll fax a quote as soon as you can. You should be able to get them something in writing within a few hours. Don't worry, they'll wait.

Rules of Thumb

Some clients will press you for an "ballpark" cost while they have you on the telephone. Although the temptation is great, *avoid* giving them a cost figure. Frankly, it's impossible to come up with these kind of "ballpark" figures. Remember, you're not building washing machines. You're creating a *custom* animated sequence built around a specific set of parameters *unique* to each individual client. Asking for a ballpark figure is like asking how much the "average" Picasso painting is worth? Don't get sucked into quoting "ballpark" figures, or using "rules of thumb" to describe the costs of your custom creations.

If a potential client *insists* that you provide a "ballpark" figure, give them a price range. Make the spread wide enough to be essentially useless, "A flying logo might cost anywhere from $500 to $10,000 dollars. It's really impossible to know the cost of a custom job until I know the specifics." This kind of response lets the client know that each job is special, and that you're unable to commit to a price until you know exactly what is required. Then try to pin down the client on the parameters and offer to fax them a quote. Always emphasize the *custom* nature of your work.

Determine the Budget

The hardest thing about putting together a successful bid - one that will land you a job - is trying to figure out exactly what it's going to cost you.

You can save a lot of time preparing a workable quote if you can find out how much the client has set aside for the animation sequence. I have yet to find a client who has allocated enough money for what they wanted to accomplish. Client's have an idea that computer animation can be expensive, but most don't have any idea *how* expensive.

You could come right out and ask, "How much money you got, tough guy?" But, that approach is not likely to generate positive results. Clients are afraid to tell you how much they've budgeted, because they're afraid you'll bleed them. The fact of the matter is most inexperienced clients budget far to little for animation and effects. Chances are you'll need more than they budgeted to deliver what the project calls for.

Don't be afraid to lay your cards on the table. Tell them the truth, "Animation can be terribly expensive. But, if I know how much you've got to work with, I can design a sequence that gives you the biggest bang for the buck." Most clients will appreciate your honesty and give you an idea of the budget.

In some cases, you can tell if they've got the right budget from a description of the overall project. A client trying to produce a three-minute video pitch for a one-time sales meeting probably can't afford a $3,000 dollar logo treatment. On the other hand, if the same video was the prime tool for a nationwide sales campaign, a sizable budget would be appropriate. Ask questions that will give you details about the overall project, then suggest a figure, "Sounds like you've got about $(your guess) dollars to work with?" The client will either agree or correct you. Either way, you're in a position to structure a design concept that fits their budget. There's no sense in wasting time designing a concept they can't afford.

Submitting the Quote

Your quote should contain all of the information necessary for the client to make a decision, and you to begin work. In essence, the quote is your contract. When the client accepts your price, they accept it subject to the terms and conditions spelled out in the quote. When you draft your bid, make sure that it states clearly what you will perform in exchange for the amount specified. Each quote should include the following information:

(1.) **Date.** This is the date that the quote is submitted.

(2.) **Contact information.** Your name, company name, telephone, fax, and email should be listed at the top of the page.

(3.) **Client information.** The client's name, company, telephone, fax, and other contact information should be listed immediately below your contact information.

(4.) **Job.** The name of the job being quoted.

(5.) **Description.** A two or three line description of the project.

(6.) **Overview.** A textual description of the concept, design, or idea of the animated sequence. This should be fairly descriptive, although you don't have to spell out every detail that will go into the final animation. In essence, this is a text-based version of the storyboard. Use as many words as necessary to adequately describe the intended sequence.

(7.) **Length.** The exact number of shots and length in seconds of the intended project. Don't use vague terms like "completion of the show" or "approximately thirty seconds." Spell it out, *exactly*.

(8.) **Schedule.** Indicate how many days - or weeks - it will take to complete the project. If the exact deadline date is known, put it here. Approval dates (if known) can also be listed here.

(9.) **Technical.** Any special technical requirements or responsibilities should be listed here. For example, if the client is responsible for the cost of digital transfers and tape stock, say so here.

(10.) **Cost.** This is the final, all inclusive cost of the services to be rendered. Bold this line item, so the client can find it easily.

(11.) **Terms.** So far, you have spelled out *what* you will do. Now, you'll dictate the conditions under which you will work. This section should contain the following:

(a) **Payment Schedule.** Here, you tell the client how you will be paid. (i.e. Half payment in advance, balance due upon delivery.) You should note that the "Cost figure includes all expenses." This reassures the client that there are no surprises. Also include the statement: "Any alterations to this agreement could require a renegotiation of the quoted price." This lets the client know that major revisions to the concept may alter the price you quoted. Of course, it is your prerogative to decide if the suggested change merits altering the price.

(b) **Property rights.** Include the following statement: "All production materials, with the exception of the final rendered images, remain the property of (your company)." This tells the client that *only* the final images are being sold for the price quoted. Clients who want to own the models, scene files, texture maps, and other elements that went into the making of the final images should pay additional fees.

(c) **Effective dates.** Include the following statement: "All prices are effective for thirty (30) days from this date." This prevents the client from holding you to a quote long after the price is practical. You can adjust the effective time period to suit your preference.

Don't sell yourself short

One final thought about pricing your work - *don't sell yourself short*. First timers naturally feel uneasy about placing a price tag on their newly acquired skills. That's okay. The uncertainty you experience in those first few jobs is actually *a part of the process*.

"In the beginning, you should charge for your services with confidence," says Will Vinton Studios senior technical director Steve Bailey. "I know it's really hard. When I first started freelancing, it seemed like every job was a new thing that I had never done before. So I would think, 'How can I charge all this money for something that I don't know if I can do or not?' But, the thing I found is that *every* job is like that. Even here at the studio.

"For instance, we had this episode of *The PJ's* where I had to use Hypervoxels to create this burning ball of sewer gas that goes through the sewer system. So, we were having a breakdown meeting and talking about how we're going to shoot the shot on the stage and what kind of elements I'm going to get. So, it's all kind of theoretical until you actually do it. You just hope that with all the experience you've had over the years, that if something goes wrong you'll spot it before you get too far down the road.

"So, I'd say you never get away from that whole seat of the pants feeling; doing something you've never done before. That's how the whole business works. You always find yourself saying, 'Well, let's try it and see what happens.' "

Losing the Bid

Whether a client accepts your bid hinges on a variety of factors - many of them outside of your control. You might lose out to a competitor because of a pre-established relationship, a lower bid, or simply because the project was dropped. Don't try to second guess why you didn't land a project. If your quote is rejected, *ask the client directly* why your quote wasn't accepted. You'll always get an answer. Whatever the response, always ask, "Is there any *other* reason?" This is a way of searching out the truth of the matter.

Many times, people are afraid to tell you the *real* reason they awarded a project to someone else. This usually happens when the decision was not based on your quote, but outside factors. Your mission is to find out if your quote was rejected based on its own merits, or on factors outside of your control.

If your quote was rejected based on outside factors, you may be given a fictitious excuse for the rejection. (Nobody wants to admit they based a decision on outside influences.) However prepared the client may be for your initial question, they are rarely prepared to offer a *second* reason. If the client offers a second reason for the rejection, it is likely the *real* reason your quote was turned down. That's because, people feel compelled to respond to a question put to them. When people offer excuses, they almost never prepare two. Your request for a second reason catches them off guard. Under the circumstances, most people will blurt out the truth the second time around. If they reiterate their *first* answer the second time around, you can safely assume you've gotten the true reason for the rejection. Try it, it works!

If the reason for the rejection is something you did, make an adjustment in your next project quote. Refine your approach until your success rate begins to outweigh the rejections. Then, stick to the formula!

Winning the Bid

Congratulations! With a winning bid comes the responsibility of making sure you develop a happy client who wants to come back to you with future work. The best way to assure this outcome is to approach each project with a professional, take-charge attitude.

Taking Charge

Don't be timid when it comes to working with clients. Nothing will undermine a client's confidence in you faster than timidity. In the long run, the only thing any client really wants is to be reassured. They want to feel that they chose a vendor who will make *them* look good.

Freelancers who take a back seat to their client in the early stages of a project will find themselves fighting for control of that project for the duration of the relationship. This is the ultimate nightmare - one in which the freelancer has become nothing more than an off-site employee.

The reason is simple: *fear*. The client is *afraid* you don't know what you're doing. They're *afraid* their decision to hire you is going to backfire into a horrific failure that will reflect badly on them. You've got to eliminate that fear *immediately*, if you hope to retain the control and respect that is necessary to survive as a freelance animator. Put the client at ease by taking charge of the project from the minute the bid is awarded. Remember, *the client is waiting for you to tell them what to do.*

On the other hand, don't smother your client with your commanding presence. Easy up a bit, and offer a balance. If you take charge and ignore their input, they begin thinking, 'Why am I even here? This guy is doing whatever he wants to do.' You've got to instill confidence in the client that you're capable of delivering their vision, and making their vision better than they believed possible. And then, let them take credit for it.

Present an Overview

As soon as you learn you've gotten the project, lay out the stages of the project in broad strokes. This can be done over the telephone. In the course of describing each step, *let the client know where they're involved.* This overview should include three phases:

(1.) **Storyboards.** Tell the client this the first stage of the process, "I'll draw up a storyboard and bring them by for your approval." Set a date for a meeting to approve the storyboard. Don't wait for the client to pick a date (this gives them control), instead suggest a date of your own, "What does your schedule look like Tuesday?" Don't pick a date too far away. Keep the client excited by picking a date one day or so away. If the date you suggest won't work, ask the client to pick a date within a range, "How about sometime between Wednesday and Friday?" Remember, the person asking questions maintains control of the conversation. You want to let the client know you're in charge. If the storyboards already exist, start with the next phase.

(2.) **Wireframe preview.** Tell the client that the next approval stage is the wireframe preview. This will allow the client to see the animation in motion and get a sense of timing before a final render. You'll also show them a color preview (or still frame) which will allow them to approve the color scheme. Set a date for this approval now. The idea is to give the client a sense of how the schedule will lay out and how the project will come to completion. You'll need to emphasize that the wireframe preview is the *final* approval stage for the client. Any changes after this point will result in increased costs.

(3.) **Final render.** Tell the client that after the wireframe approval, the animation will go to final render. You won't know exactly how long it will take to do the final render until after the color previews have been done. But, you can give the client an estimate now, and suggest a completion date, "I should be able to deliver next Thursday or Friday." Your language here lets them know that a firm date will be given at a later time.

By the end of the telephone conversation you should have an approval schedule and a good idea when you will deliver.

Remember, for most clients this is a new experience. It's easy for them to become afraid and unsure. When clients become frightened, they grab control. You can easily prevent that from happening by fulfilling the role of leader. Simply hold their hand and walk them through the process. Don't be intimidated by their corporate title. After all, *you're* the animation expert! You'll find that clients are excited by the prospect of dabbling in a little Hollywood magic, and willing to do just about anything you tell them.

Working with clients

Working with clients can be a pleasurable experience, or the worst nightmare of your life. Fortunately, the experience - good or bad - is largely in *your* hands. You may not be able to control the client, but you can control your *attitude*.

Clients come in all shapes and sizes. At times, you're sure to encounter clients who are bossy, obnoxious, forgetful, arrogant, and just plain stupid. Learning how to *react* to the various personalities you'll meet is the key ingredient that will make or break your business.

Although it's easy to explode under the kind of trying conditions that revolve around any business, keep in mind that your freelance relationship with any one client is only *temporary*. When the project is over, you're in a position to choose whether it's worth returning to that client for future work. Always remember, *you're in the driver's seat*.

No matter how troublesome a client can be, you can always find *something* to like about them. Concentrate on that trait. Say to yourself, "At least I can like *this* about the guy." Then, try to communicate with them on that level.

"I don't ever start a project where I assume the client is going to be a nightmare," says Digital Muse's Matt Merkovich. "I always assume the client is going to be great. I look for something about the client that I like, so that when I deal with the client, I'm dealing with them in a friendly manner. You'll avoid so many problems just by taking that point of view. Anyone who tells you contrary is just jaded because they don't know how to deal with clients in the first place. Remember, there's no such thing as bad clients, only people dealing badly with clients."

In the end, learn to adjust your attitude to meet the client's needs. You'll find it's easier to overlook those personality quirks if you keep focused on the task at hand. You've been hired to perform a task, and to deliver your best efforts. Do it. Don't get caught up in personality conflicts that jeopardize the project or the perception of your work habits. A bad reputation lingers long after the act has been forgotten. Protect your reputation at all costs. You never want to put yourself in a position where someone can justifiably question your work performance. How well you perform is the product you are selling. Don't allow a disreputable client to damage your product, by suckering you into a confrontation. It's easy to deliver top quality work under ideal conditions. The real test of your business ethics comes when you're challenged to rise above the fray, and deliver outstanding work under extremely hostile conditions.

Few people can pass this test, but those who do are destined to prosper in a business that consumes people like no other.

Getting the job done

From your first meeting to your last, *the client is always right*. When push comes to shove, the client should get what they want. After all, they're paying the bill. That doesn't mean you can't influence their decision.

Always remember that *you* are the animation expert. It's up to *you* to do whatever it takes to deliver a quality product, which may include convincing the client that their idea is not right for the job. Foundation Imaging's P.J. Foley knows how important it is to stick to your gut instinct.

"Back when I was just starting out freelancing, a client wanted a logo done, but demanded that I put his logo of blue, clear Lucite on a purple, nebulous galaxy. I tried to tell him he would never be able to see it - especially with the limitations of video. But, he wouldn't listen, and I gave in. It took eleven days to render the final sequence and the result was exactly what I expected. The client, of course, was very unhappy. I learned a valuable lesson. Don't let the client bulldoze you into their idea simply because they like it. You have to sell them on what will work. Trust your instincts."

Communication

The key ingredient when dealing with clients is *communication*. Most client battles can be averted by simply making sure both you and the client have a clear understanding of what is expected and what can be delivered. Achieving a meeting of the minds is not always as easy as it sounds.

"Probably the worst client nightmare is when the client doesn't really know what they want," says Digital Muse executive producer and veteran animator John Gross. "On the other hand, they usually know what they *don't* want when you show them. (laughs) They don't know what they want and they really don't have the means to communicate to you properly as an artist. It drives up the frustration level for everybody - for the client and the artist. If you're having a hard time dealing with the client, what you need to do is bring in additional people. In our case, we bring in the producer of the project and sit down with the artist and the client and solve the problem. You need to get the client to clarify their position by answering yes and no questions. You asked them, 'Do you mean by this, we should do X?' Through that process, the truth of what they really want will come out."

Being an effective communicator means you'll need to become a part-time psychologist if you hope to avoid communication disasters.

"The worst nightmare is when you're discussing something and everyone *thinks* they understand," explains Kirk Kelley, director for Will Vinton Studios, "and then you send them the final version and it's not *anything* like what they were thinking. And so your words didn't convey your idea. The way to avoid that is to talk through it very clearly using other examples of things if you can - things you've seen that are close to what you're talking about - that's helpful. Point to well known movies that conjure up something very specific in their mind, so they've got a visual of what you're describing. If there is any kind of hesitation in their voice, you have to kind of read between the lines and question, 'What is that hesitation about?' Keep asking questions. Especially on the telephone, where you can't see their face. I find that asking questions on conference calls is really important. But the biggest key is to *listen*. Listen to what they're saying. Listen to the spaces between what they're saying, and try to figure out the dynamics of the other parties involved. If one person speaks, ask yourself, 'Are they speaking for the group, or are they just providing an opinion that won't be held by the group on the other end?' Try to figure out what it all means. To a degree, you have to be a psychologist with really good communication skills."

Ultimately, communicating effectively with your client is a responsibility that you - as a freelancer - must carry.

"Your client has no burden other than to pay you," instructs Digital Muse's Matt Merkovich. "That's it. Everything else falls on your shoulders - to communicate with the client, find out exactly what he wants, get a really good picture of what he wants, and then get your software to do what he wants. And if your software can't do what he wants, get different software. But, get your client happy. If your client wants *Jurassic Park* and he's only got $5,000 dollars, then your client just needs to be educated. But you can still deal with that client. You just need to tell your client, 'Look, they did *Jurassic Park* for several million dollars. You've got five thousand. But, let's try to work it out where we can get you something that you'll be happy with, that will be in the same vein of what you're trying to accomplish.' Your client will love you. Then, you're the hero."

Managing client changes

Your primary objective is to *manage* the money you've been allotted, and come out ahead. If you find you're continually losing money, you don't have a business, you've got an expensive hobby. Believe me, it's very easy to find you're over budget on complicated animation projects. The surest way to get into financial trouble is to paint yourself into a corner with client changes.

There was a running joke among the production staff at CBS/Fox Video over the unending wave of changes that seemed to burden every project. We got use to calling ourselves the "changemasters," because the creative concepts would swing like a pendulum from day to day. Although it was easy to blame the client in those situations, the real problem lay with our own producers, who failed to control the project.

Offer choices

The easiest way to steer a project is by offering the client choices. Clients are naturally hesitant to commit to an idea or concept. More often than not, they're looking for approval - some sign from you that they're making the right decision.

As the animation producer, it's up to you to take control of the decision making process. You can do this by offering suggestions, "Plan *A* will be quicker, but Plan *B* will look better. Which would you prefer?" The client is now thrust into the role of decision maker - a role everyone relishes. But, since both choices are of your own making, it doesn't matter which one is selected. Either way, you win.

This is an effective management tool because it allows the client to have *ownership* of the project, while giving you *control*. This is the key to minimizing overages in time and money. Remember, you've agreed to produce a project for a specific amount of money. You can't afford to give control of the project to the client under those terms. You can, however, allow them to make decisions under very controlled circumstances. Here's how you can maintain control as the project progresses through each phase:

Storyboards

Offer variations on a concept as you present your storyboards. You can illustrate each variation with multiple storyboards, or, better yet, present the best (your favorite) option and talk your way through the variations. This approach can subtly sway the clients to your vision, simply because it will be difficult for them to envision anything but the concept you've sketched. Your variations on the proposed theme offers them choices, but only within the guidelines of your predetermined concept. Think of it as *controlled* choices.

Wireframe Previews

This is the phase in which your client will exercise their right to make the most choices and changes. When clients have an opportunity to make a change, they'll invariably do so - especially if it's their *last chance* to do so.

You'll need to keep a tight rein on their choices, or you'll find yourself working long hours redesigning the animation for next to nothing. If you've followed the storyboard closely, there are only a few things that clients can legitimately alter:

(1.) **Timing**. The speed at which an animation unfolds is tough to visualize based on a storyboard sketch. So, be prepared to fine tune the animation after clients get a look at the wireframe preview. The best way to avoid long hours of reworking a complex animation sequence is to build it in modules. Break down complex actions into smaller nuggets that can be tweaked independently.

Most software programs allow you to set up your animation in blocks that can be assembled into more complicated motions. Take advantage of this feature, and build each major movement as a separate action. This will allow you to make minor changes in speed and position with a minimum of effort.

Another way to offer choices (and save time) is to playback the wireframe preview at various speeds. This gives the client a good idea of what the animation would look like if it unfolded at half or double the speed at which it was conceived.

Most software programs allow you to playback a pre-rendered wireframe sequence at various speeds without re-rendering. If yours doesn't, pre-render your preferred sequence at half, as well as double-speed, in advance. *Don't offer to show these altered speeds unless the client raises the issue*.

(2.) **Color and Texture**. When it comes to surfaces and backgrounds for your animated objects, offer two or three color choices or textures.

"Do you prefer the yellow-gold, or the orange-gold?" "Do you like the burlap background, or the brickface?" Keep the choices offered to less than three. Offering more than three adds confusion, and makes it harder for the client to decide. Above all, never offer a choice you can't live with.

Pre-render each color choice as a still image. Pick a representative frame of the animation that captures all of the objects in question, and render it as a sample. Show the client the same frame, with each of the choices. This gives them a way to compare the color and textures with each other.

(3.) **Color previews.** As computer processors get faster, the opportunity to render fully colored and textured previews becomes more practical. Although it may seem preferable to show the client the best available preview possible, the practice can work against you. Fully colored and textured previews have a "finished" look to them, even though motions, textures, and other components have not been polished. You risk having your work judged on this incomplete preview, which may give your client the impression that you're an amateur - or worse - untalented.

People make judgments based on what they see everyday on television. Clients are no different. Unless your color "preview" will stand up against the best television has to offer (and most previews, by nature, won't), you should avoid showing it to the client.

A wireframe preview has an unfinished look to it. The message the client gets is that it is still in an unfinished state. As such, the client will be willing to overlook a lot of the "bumps" your work will have at this stage. If you *must* show a color preview, turn off the image effects that are added to a polished sequence (antialiased effects, lensflares, etc.), and render it with running frame counts and a superimposed title, such as: "Preview Sequence No.15." These are visual clues that tell the client this is a work in progress.

Remember to always *limit* the amount of choices you give a client, and only offer them a choice when the amount of work it will create is inconsequential. If you bid the project correctly, you should have plenty of leeway to make the kind of changes that make clients happy.

Final Render

Just because it's called "final" render, doesn't mean there won't be changes. Some clients (usually the ones that can afford to) just can't help massaging the animation one more time.

If it's a minor color change, or an alteration in motion that requires little more than machine time, let it go. Especially if you can still hit their deadline without extra effort. Machine time is the least expensive part of the process. After all, you can sleep while the machine hums away, right?

However, if you find a client who wants to rework large amounts of an animated sequence at a cost to your time and effort, then by all means charge them accordingly. Some clients don't care, and are willing to pay.

Delivering the goods

When you're ready to deliver the final sequence, call the client and let them know the job is done. Make arrangements to deliver and receive your final payment. To facilitate the final payment ask the client if they want you to fax over a copy of the invoice. Some clients will just ask you for the final amount, and have you bring the invoice when you deliver.

Invoices

Make sure the invoice includes the following:

(1.) **Your contact information**. Your name, address, telephone number, fax number, and email address.

(2.) **Invoice number**. This is a number you assign to the invoice to keep your records straight. For example, you might use a coded version of the invoice date: MonthDayYear, followed by the invoice number for that day. (i.e. 122999001 represents the first invoice (001) for 12/29/99)

(3.) **Customer Purchase Order number**. Include the number assigned to the project, if one is given. Type "verbal," is none was provided.

(4.) **Invoice Date**. This is the date the invoice is submitted. Usually the date of delivery.

(5.) **Customer contact information**. The name, address, and telephone number of the company the job was sold to. The contact person (your client contact) should be added on a separate line below this.

(6.) **Terms of payment**. Use the phrase, "Net on receipt." This tells the client that payment is due as soon as they receive the invoice.

(7.) **Job description**. List the title of the job and/or a brief description. (i.e. 3D Animation: M&M's 30-second spot, "Run")

(8.) **Amount due**. This is what they owe you. **Bold** and star (***) this entry to draw attention.

(9.) **Payable information**. At the bottom of the invoice, add the line: "Make checks payable to: (Your Company Name)." This lets the accountant know who to make the check out to.

(10.) **Questions**. Under item #9, add the line: "Direct questions to: (Your Name and telephone number)." This provides a contact for questions pertaining to the invoice.

Take a bow

There usually isn't any "wrap" party at the end of a project. In fact, most jobs are delivered without much fanfare. Producers are usually too busy trying to make a deadline to do much more than thank you for a job well done.

However, you should take the time to write a letter thanking the client for choosing you. You don't have to write more than a few lines, but make sure you let the client know that you enjoyed working with them and hope they'll keep you in mind for their next project. Few people bother to give thanks, so a short note will be remembered.

Chapter 10:
Building Your Business

There are clients worth getting involved with, and others you'll want to avoid like the plague. Learning to spot the difference requires experience.

Most newcomers to the business gain their experience the hard way. If you follow the advice in the following pages, you can avoid many of the land mines that plague other beginners. It won't keep you from stumbling altogether, but it can save you from major disaster.

Client myths

There are plenty of myths that clients tend to foist on newcomers to the animation business. These are sayings and promises that - when believed - can put you behind the eight ball. Here's a list of the most common client myths - in no particular order - and the real truth of the matter:

Myth #1. "If you'll do this job for half price, I've got lot's more down the road." When you're just starting out, this is the one you'll hear the most. It's also the biggest whopper. What you *think* they're saying is, "If you do this job for less than you're rate, I can get you lots of work at your regular rates." But, what they're *really* saying is, "If you'll do this at half price, I've got a lot more work you can do at half price."

Clients who want work done for half price, will *always* want work done for half price. You'll never bump them up to a realistic rate. As soon as you hold firm to your terms, they'll replace you with someone else who'll bow to this game just like you did. Chances are, they're billing *their* client for the full rate and pocketing *your* profit.

It's easy to get sucked into this deal, especially when you're starting out. You'll justify it with a series of rationalizations - none of which hold water under careful scrutiny:

(a) **"Some money is better than no money."** This is the first one you'll think of. You're hungry and working beats the hell out of not working. The problem with this thinking is that you're not in business to *work*. You're in business to *earn a profit*. Working at half your rate guarantees that you'll earn no profit. You've simply agreed to spend your valuable time working for nothing.

You're better off, pulling your belt tighter and spending what time you have making contacts and trolling for a real paying job. In fact, it'll really frost you when you have to turn down a paying job, because you're tied up on a project that's paying you next to nothing. Believe me, it happens all the time.

(b) **"I can always put the animation on my demo reel."** Perhaps. But nine times out of ten, you won't want to. About halfway through the project, you'll realize what a chump you are for taking this job. Your attitude will begin to affect your work, resulting in a sequence that's not your best effort. You'll end up keeping it off your reel, which means the only thing you got out of the deal was the money. That's when you'll say to yourself, "What money?"

Never do a project just for your reel. If you're going to do that, you'd be better off to work on a project of your *own* creation. You'll be more enthusiastic, and the final results will show it. When working for others, charge a fair rate. If they're unable to pay, *invest your spare time in yourself* by either looking for work, or developing your skills. *Never give your time away to someone else for free.*

(c) **"They might come through with a real paying job down the road."** It'll *never* happen - guaranteed. The reason is simple. Respectable clients who know the value of an animation sequence will never expect to pay well below rate. It's only the unscrupulous clients who expect animators to drop their rates to half, for a "promise" of future work.

Think about it. Would that work at your local grocery store? ("Give me these groceries at half price, and I promise to buy lots more at full price down the road.") Face it, it's a con. The only thing you've guaranteed, is a client who'll return to you for *another* half-price deal. As soon as you try to get a fair rate, they'll run in search of the next sucker. *Don't bite on this one.*

Myth #2. "If you do this job on spec, I'm certain we'll sell the project." A spec ("speculation") job is one you're doing for free - start to finish - in the hopes that your client will sell his project. If he does, so the tale goes, you'll get paid. The promise usually includes a handsome reward consisting of additional high paying work related to the "project." This type of come-on never pays off.

"I don't do spec work," declares digital effects supervisor Matt Merkovich. "I'm in Hollywood. Everybody out here has got a project. There are so many projects, movies and show ideas that people are trying to get off the ground and get on the air. What makes any of them any more special than any other one? The people who are successful? They don't do things that way. I'll only do things the way people who are already successful do things. If the guys that are successful don't do spec crap, then I won't either. It's stupid. It's a big waste of time. If you spent the same amount of effort you're going spend on a spec job, and took that energy and effort and dedicated it to laying off more demo reels, boxing them up, and mailing them out to companies who have work and actually have money for you, what do you think would happen? It's common sense. Which approach is more productive? If you know you have a demo reel that pulls and will get you work, then you're stupid to do spec work."

Spec work should not be confused with an animation "test," which is occasionally requested as a sample of your capability or to demonstrate an effect for a specific project. Your hope is that the client will hire you to do the project once you've demonstrated your ability. This is a pretty common practice in the animation business, but one that you - as a freelancer - will find hard to payoff.

Post production studios and larger animation houses are in a better position to do test work simply because they're already committed to a significant investment in overhead each month. Even if there is no paying work coming in, they've still got a payroll to meet. Rather than pay staff people for nothing, a test job offers the *chance* to land a big project at no additional cost to the studio. However, as a freelancer, you don't have that same luxury. An investment of your efforts in a test job actually robs you of the only commodity you have - time. And frankly, you can't afford to tie up your time (which could be used looking for paying work) in the hope of landing a job down the road.

"If it's the difference between doing a test for the sequel to *A Bug's Life*, and a logo that'll make you $5,000 dollars - do the logo that'll make you money," advises Merkovich. "I don't care if it's a test for Steven Spielberg. Do the logo that makes you money now. If you follow that rule - generally - I think you'll do much better. Hey, you *might* lose a big job working for Steven Spielberg. But, you know what? You *definitely* lost five grand."

The fact of the matter is most test jobs *don't* turn into big contracts. Many times, test work is used to browbeat larger production houses into lowering their prices. For instance, I was asked to create some test footage for a national television campaign. The job involved creating a computer effect with live action footage. The effort was time consuming, but the results spectacular. Despite a well positioned project bid, the job was awarded to a major west coast effects house. I later learned that the agency used my bid and test footage to get the west coast house to lower their price fifteen percent. They did, and got the job.

Does this happen all the time? Not at all. In fact, some animators have made good use of test footage opportunities.

"I can show a client looking to do an animated hornet an incredible, animated bumble bee on my reel," freelance animator Brad Carvey explains, "and if somebody else has a mediocre hornet on their reel, they'll get the job every time. That's because the client just doesn't understand that if I can do a really great bumble bee, I can do a really great hornet. So, if I really want the job - I'll always try to do a test, because it's my feeling that a client just can't make the leap from a demo reel to the specifics of what they want. Whatever I do, it's never longer than five seconds. A lot of times it's just a still. Maybe it's a frozen model, but the camera is moving around so they can see it. The danger is that if you give them too much, they think that is the best you can do. If you give them a decent model and you tell them that it doesn't have a final texture, or if you give them a decent looking model and another model that has a final texture on it, then maybe they can bridge the gap. It gets down to guess work."

As enticing as a large project may be, test work rarely pays off. If you simply can't resist the temptation - and *must* roll the dice on a test job - be sure to get your costs covered with a minimal fee. Charging a client for materials or a small labor fee is not unreasonable or unheard of. In any case, let the client know that test work is secondary to paid projects. If one comes along, they should understand that the test work will go to the back burner.

"Everyone's had to do test work when it was appropriate," says Station X's Grant Boucher. "We've done tests for Warner Brothers, DreamWorks, and many other studios. And we've been paid for them. Now, the price may not have been at full rate - for a test it's usually at a substantial discount - but we've been paid for it. It sets up a precedent. And quite frankly, at the very high end you do very little free tests. We say, 'Hey, look. We're just like any other company. We have to pay staff. We'll give you a good rate, but you have to pay for the test.' And it also proves that they're serious.

"Now, if somebody comes to you and says, 'You have to do this test at half-rate,' you've got to judge the relationship. If you've got your labor costs covered, then it's really a win-win. You may not be making a profit, but you're building a relationship with the client, showing off your best work, and - if you do your job well - you've got something great for the demo reel. And in the best of all worlds, you get the job. There is a time and a place to do a test, and you really have to judge how serious they are based on their reputation. There are a lot of hustlers out there - especially in Hollywood - who'll say, 'Oh, do this for me and I'll do this, this, and this.' You can qualify them by getting them to cover your costs. If they refuse to pay up front, what makes you think they'll have the money at the back end?

"The biggest problem you'll face is that clients want to treat you like they're paying you full rate. (laughs) If you're doing something as a test, you need to demand some things in return, like a flexible schedule - the ability to shift your gears if necessary. If a paying job comes in and I'm doing your test job, I'm sorry, your delivery is going to slip. If you want to pay for the slot, you're going to get the privileges for that - we're going to deliver on time, we're going to do everything you ask, and we're going to make it happen. But, if I'm doing this as a test for you, then some things are going to happen - I'm going to cover my expenses, and make sure I secure some flexibility."

Myth #3. "I can't pay any money up front, but I'll pay in full on delivery." This amounts to asking for credit. The risk is that you'll complete the work, and the client will refuse to pay or want to extend the payment terms further, "I still can't pay you now, but I'll pay as soon as my client pays *me*." Now, you've put yourself in a situation where you must release the completed animation to the client in order to get paid. As we discussed earlier, once you release the product you're at the mercy of the client to pay when - and *if* - they decide to pay you.

Remember, you're not a bank. Don't give credit under any circumstances. Your payment terms (half up front, balance on delivery; or one-third up front, one-third midpoint, one-third on delivery) should be considered *non-negotiable*.

To insure that you get paid, make sure the client is financially vested in the project. Without some client money up front, you're the only one risking anything. The amount you receive up front (one-half, or one-third) is usually enough to cover your out of pocket costs. If the client backs out of the deal, you haven't lost anything. *I've never seen a client back out of a project they've sunk money into*. Never begin a project without money up front.

Myth #4. "I can give you half up front, but I need 30 days on the final payment." This is another variation of the credit request. In this version, your out of pocket costs are covered, but you'll likely wait more than thirty days to get paid - *if at all*. That's because in this situation you've got to give up the collateral (the completed animation) before you get paid in full. This is a bad risk (as any banker will tell you).

Most clients who ask for credit will claim that they must wait for their client to pay *them*. That may be true, but from a business standpoint that's really not *your* problem. In essence, they're passing their financial problems to you. Remember, your client's financial agreements are not *your* burden. Paying you on time, at the terms you negotiated, is their responsibility. Don't let them pass the buck. The easiest way to avoid this situation is to *never give credit*.

Myth #5. "If we find we're putting too may effects on the front end of the show, we'll either taper them off on the back end of the show or find more money." The reality is that the client will want even more effects toward the end of the season. And they won't have any money left. The obvious way to avoid the situation is to anticipate it in your original budget. When you work out your budget make sure you're making enough money to cover the cost of the additional shots. Because the sorry fact is, you'll probably be doing them anyway.

"Once you know what to anticipate most horror stories are averted," says Foundation Imaging's Jeff Scheetz. "You have to make a lot of assumptions on the front end about what it's really going to be like. Even though they're telling you, 'You can reuse footage. These things are going to become stock shots, so you won't have to worry about that. It's going to save you a day.' And so you figure out on your own that what they're saying doesn't really matter."

To avoid assumptions and misunderstandings, always spell out the *exact* number of shots (or the *exact* length) in your contract terms.

Myth #6. "It's just a minor change." The truth is, there is no such thing as a *minor* change.

"Clients tend to believe that because we're working with computers, that it's all fast and all powerful," explains Rhythm & Hues animator Lyndon Barrois. "They think we're just pressing buttons and changing whole performances. (laughs) It's just not true. I mean, this stuff takes time. So, a lot of times clients have to be told, 'We can't do what you're asking in the time you've allotted. It's going to cost you X amount more.' Because, that's the truth of it. I can't spend three weeks animating something and then all of a sudden a client decides, 'What if we want to do it this way,' and I have a week to deliver. Well, that just doesn't fly. If it's something small maybe that's doable. But, a lot of times, those changes require a lot of re-animation and we just don't have the time. So, you have to tell them, 'Yea, we can do that - absolutely! You won't get it in a week, and it'll cost you so many thousand more.' Then, they'll change their tunes, 'Oh, well. We can live with it the way it is.' "

Myth #7. "I think it looks great." You usually hear this during an approval process when you're really hoping to hear any last minute criticism, so that you can make corrections. But then, on the final day of rendering they'll say, 'One more thing, could we change this.' And of course, the answer at that point is, 'Well, no. The time to do that was quite some time ago.' So when they say, 'It looks great,' what they really mean is it looks great to them, *then*. Clients will always look for an opportunity to make changes. The only thing you can do, is be professional, explain the way things are, and hope you have a rational client who can be pragmatic about things.

"I worked on *Spawn*," remembers Digital Muse's Bruce Branit, "and did the modeling, lighting, and animation in about four days - less than two weeks before the movie opened. They were just throwing shots at everyone in Hollywood. At the end of the production process they were still asking for wholesale changes. And what they were really doing is they were trying to get as much as they could until you said, 'I can't do anymore.' And then they said, 'You know, it looks great.' I think a lot of clients are that way. If you're looking for a car and the salesman keeps coming down on price, you're not going to stop him until he says, 'This is it.' So, you have to understand that clients have needs too, and they want to keep squeezing it out until you tell them they can't. And that's your job to say that. It's not your job to throw up your hands and say, 'This guy's asking for everything!' You *do* have a place to say, 'This is *really* all we can do.' So, don't be afraid to give them your honest appraisal of the situation."

Myth #8. "The guy that writes the check isn't here right now." This is the one you'll hear when the client is trying to get the master tape from you without paying the final installment. The client has usually insisted that they need the tape delivered on a specific day and time, you show up, and they're not prepared to pay you - but *insist* on getting the tape.

"That's my favorite client myth," chuckles Digital Muse's Matt Merkovich. "I'll say, 'Well, I thought the tape was real important to have here today?' 'Oh, it really is.' 'Well, you can see the tape's done. If you need it, you should probably call up the guy that writes the check and get him over here so he can sign the check.' 'He's not available.' 'Oh, well that's really bad. Here's our contract...' And then they give a big spiel on how this is not a good way to do business, blah-blah-blah. You know immediately that this is a client that you should never work for again. And *don't* give them their tape! And you know what? Every single time that this has happened - and it's happened three times out of the hundreds and hundreds of clients I've had - the guy that signs the check miraculously shows up, they sign your check and shove it at you begrudgingly. That's when I run to the bank. One time I called the bank and verified that the funds were there. And *then*, gave them their tape. I've never once in my entire career, not been paid for something. I know a lot of people that can't say that. Take my advice. There's no reason for anyone to ever say, 'Well, okay. I'll make this exception for you because I like you.' This is show *business*. Show-*business*. People don't put enough emphasis on the business part of it."

Myth #9. "It's easier to fix it in post." This is the one you'll hear from clients who don't understand the complexities of computer effects - which includes just about everyone.

"The truth of the matter is that we *are* post and we don't find it particularly easy," laughs Rhythm & Hues' Pauline Ts'o. "Avoiding that mindset is really a matter of educating the entire industry as to what is adequate pre-production, and what is efficient pre-visualization. Some effects supervisors and directors can do it better than others. Some directors just naturally want to see every single possibility before they decide, and they'll never change. But others will slowly learn that the more they nail down in the beginning - which they all hate to do - the less expensive it will be. That's the producers job. A lot of that is setting up client expectations about how much flexibility is reasonable in our eyes in terms of what budget we've been given. The key is talking to the client as often as possible, so there is no surprises or misunderstandings."

Myth #10. "What do you think?" You'll hear this from most clients at some point during the creative process. The truth of the matter is they don't really care what you think, they already have something specific in mind. That doesn't mean you can't influence their decision.

"The trick is to make them feel like your idea is *their* idea," says Kirk Kelley, director for Will Vinton Studios. "That's the key to working with clients. You have to put your ego aside and make it feel like they're coming up with ideas. You take a piece of something they said and say, 'Oh, that's a good idea. So if we took what you're saying and did this...,' and then you put a slightly different spin on it and make it more like what you were proposing. Just start with the base of their idea."

Rising above crowd

Developing a successful business is like climbing a ladder. At the bottom rungs, you tend to encounter the worst of the lot. That's because you're just learning the ropes. It's easy for people to take advantage of your naiveté. The disreputable clients tend to gravitate to the newcomers. If you let them, they will take advantage of you until you either wiseup and move on, or they put you out of business. Learn to trust the advice in this book, and you'll keep from getting buried in the early stages of your business.

As you acquire more confidence and skill, your client base will change. You'll encounter fewer disreputable clients, and move toward bigger, better paying projects. This is no accident. *The best clients control the best jobs.* That's because the reputable clients have learned to deal with only the most reliable people. Their experience and business savvy protects them from the bottom feeders that pollute the industry. They've climbed high enough on the ladder to rise above the worst of the lot. That's what you must do.

When you climb high enough on the ladder, success will begin to flow your way. You'll find the best people seeking you out. You'll find them willing to help you, because they recognize that *you've learned to do what it takes to be successful.* You'll be invited to bid on the most desirable projects. You'll make contacts you never thought possible. Your profits will soar. You'll work less and earn more than ever before.

Remember, *success breeds success.*

Building a client base

A reliable, and loyal client base is the key to building a solid foundation for your business. When you encounter a reputable client, cultivate them. Get them to always think of you, when they have animation needs.

Once you've got a solid client, don't smother them. Keep in touch, but don't make them feel like your livelihood depends solely on them. Remember, *you don't need any one client.*

I've seen freelance animators build their business around a single large client. For a while, things can look pretty rosy, and before you know it you start to think you don't need anyone else. This is a big mistake. Business climates change - often! You can bet that big corporations don't need *you* to stay in business. Don't get lulled into relying on them for your cash flow. You need to be able to walk away from any *one* client, and stay in business.

Build wide, then deep

To insure your success, cultivate many clients simultaneously. Build your business wide, then deep. Develop at least ten reputable clients that you're servicing regularly. Then, look for people they know.

Your business will never see its potential if you limit yourself to people you know personally. After all, there are only so many hours in the day, and you can't be everywhere at once. Let your client base speak for you. Let them sell others on how good you are. Ask your clients to refer other people (producers, agencies, contacts, etc.) to you. Develop relationships with three or four people that each of your clients has referred to you. This insures a solid foundation for your business. If any one of your clients drifts away (as inevitably will happen as business climates change), you can replace them with one of their other contacts.

Clients will come and go. But by cultivating your ten best clients (and having them refer people they know), you'll always have a steady flow of work.

Your most valuable commodities

Your most valuable commodity is your time. Don't waste it. Don't allow other's to waste it. Time is one thing you can't buy. With every tick of the clock, another moment slips by that you can never recover. Use your time wisely. More important, understand how important and valuable your time really is. Think of the hours you've pored into developing your animation skills, the collective knowledge you've accumulated through years of experience, and your ability to combine those two areas to produce truly creative projects.

Don't spend your time frivolously. Invest the available hours in sharpening your skills and making new contacts. Learn to respect your time. Until you do, no one else will.

The second most valuable commodity you have is your attitude. Protect it. It's tough getting up every morning to face the kind of negativity that permeates our culture. It's easy to get discouraged and to wonder if all your efforts are really worth it.

Learn to encourage and nurture a healthy, positive attitude. Read positive and motivation books on a daily basis. Stay away from naysayers and people who always focus on the negative things in life. They can't help you rise to the top. But, by succeeding, you may be able to show them a better way of life.

Acknowledgments

There are a number of people whose help made this book possible and I am very grateful for their time and cooperation.

First of all, many thanks to those who took time to talk with me about their careers and experiences: John Allardice, Supervising Visual Effects Animator, Foundation Imaging; Steve Bailey, Senior Technical Director, Will Vinton Studios; Jeff Barnes, Executive Producer, Computer Cafe; Lyndon Barrois, Character Animator, Rhythm & Hues Studios; Grant Boucher, CEO, Station X; Bruce Branit, Creative Director, Digital Muse; Brad Carvey, Freelance Animation Director; Alan Chan, Effects Supervisor, Station X; Joe Conti, Freelance Animation Director; Paul Diener, Director of Digital Production, Will Vinton Studios; Doug Dooley, Animator, Blue Sky Studios; Michael Feder, Producer, Blue Sky Studios; P.J. Foley, Supervising Visual Effects Animator, Foundation Imaging; John Follmer, Vice President and Head of Production, Metrolight Studios; John Gross, Executive Producer, Digital Muse; Karen Hillier, Professor, Visualization Sciences, Texas A&M University; Kirk Kelley, Director, Will Vinton Studios; Robert Lurye, Lighting Director, Rhythm & Hues Studios; Matt Merkovich, Effects Supervisor, Digital Muse; Chris Ohlgren, Master Animator, Will Vinton Studios; Jeff Scheetz, Supervising Animator, Foundation Imaging; Carl Scott, Graphics Coordinator, Grace & Wild Studios; Jeremie Talbot, Animator, Metrolight Studios; and Pauline Ts'o, Vice President and Co-owner, Rhythm & Hues Studios.

Thanks to all the studios and companies who were generous with supplying images for the cover art: Blue Sky Studios, Inc.; M&M/Mars, Inc.; Metrolight Studios, Inc.; Rhythm & Hues Studios; and Will Vinton Studios. Special thanks to Chris Wedge for use of the images from his Academy award-winning short, *Bunny*.

Most of all, thank you to my wife, Karen, for continued support and understanding during another book project.

Appendix A:
Animation Schools

The following is a selected list of technical, character, and software specific animation schools. Inclusion in this list does not imply any kind of endorsement, but is provided as a resource for further exploration. Many major studios list recommended schools on their websites. See *Appendix B* for a list of studios.

3D Exchange
999 E. Stanley Blvd., Suite B
Livermore, CA 94550
www.exchange3D.com
Main #: (925) 371-4500
Fax #: (925) 371-4501

Academy of Art College
79 New Montgomery
San Francisco, CA 94105
www.academyart.edu
Undergrad. Admissions: (415) 274-2200
Motion Picture: Patrick Kriwanek (415) 274-2257
Career Services: Susan Pelosi (415) 274-8675

Animation Institute of LA / Royer Studios
401 South Main Street
Los Angeles, CA 90013
www.royerstudios.com
Main #: (213) 621-9261

Art Center College of Design
1700 Lida St.
Pasadena, CA 91103
www.artcenter.edu
Undergrad. Admissions: (626)396-2373
Career Resources Dept.: (818) 396-2320

Art Institute of Pittsburgh
526 Penn Avenue
Pittsburgh, PA 15222
www.all.edu/pittsburgh.html
Main #: (800) 275-2470
Fax #: (412) 263-6667

Brown University
45 Prospect St.
Providence, RI 02912
www.brown.edu
Undergrad. Admissions: (401) 863-1000
Computer Science: (401) 863-7600
Career Services: (401) 863-3326

California Institute of Arts (CalArts)
24700 McBean Parkway
Valencia, CA 91355
www.calarts.edu
Undergrad. Admissions: (805) 255-1050
Dept. of Film & Video: (805) 253-7825
Character Animation: (805) 253-7818
Career Services: Frank Terry (805) 222-2761

California Institute of Technology
1201 E. California Boulevard
Pasadena, CA 91125
www.caltech.edu
Undergrad. Admissions: (818) 395-6341
Computer Graphics: (818) 395-2826
Computer Science: (818) 395-6244
Career Services: (818) 395-6361
Graphics Lab: www.gg.caltech.edu

California State University, Long Beach
Advanced Media Productions
1250 Bellflower Road
Long Beach, CA 90840
www.amp.csulb.edu
Main #: (562) 985-4352
Fax #: (562) 985-5292

Carnegie-Mellon University
5000 Forbes Ave.
Pittsburgh, PA 15213
www.cs.cmu.edu
Undergrad. Admissions - CS (412) 268-3609
Computer Science: (412) 268-2565
Career Services: (412) 268-2064

Cogswell Polytechnical College
1175 Bordeaux Drive
Sunnyvale, CA 94089
www.cogswell.edu
Main #: (800-264-7955
Fax #: (408) 747-0764

Columbus College of Art and Design
107 North 9 St.
Columbus, OH 43215
www.columbus.org/gcac/ccad
Main #: (614) 224-9101

Computer Arts Institute
310 Townsend Street. Suite 230
San Francisco, CA 94107
www.sirius.com/~cai
Main #: (415) 546-5242
Fax #: (415) 546-5237

Cornell University
410 Thurston Ave.
Ithaca, NY 14853
www.cornell.edu
Main #: (607) 255-2000
Computer Science: (607) 255-7316
Career Services: (607) 255-5221

De Anza College
21250 Stevens Creek Blvd.
Cupertino, CA 95014
www.deanza.fhda.edu/animation
Main #: (408) 864-8832
Fax #: (408) 864-8492

DH Institute of Media Arts
1315 3rd Street Promenade, Suite 300
Santa Monica, CA 90401
www.dhima.com
Main #: (310) 899-9377
Fax #: (310) 899-9307

Emily Carr Institute
1399 Johnston St.
Vancouver, BC
CANADA V6H 3R9
www.eciad.bc.ca
Main #: (604) 844-3800

Fashion Institute of Technology
7th Ave. & 27th St.
New York, NY 10001
www.apparel.net/fit
Main #: (212) 760-7665
Computer Graphics: (212) 760-7938

Henry Cogswell College
2802 Wetmore Avenue, Suite 100
Everett, WA 98201
www.henrycogswell.edu
Main #: (425) 258-2251
Fax #: (425) 257-0405

Inter-Dec College
2120 Sainte-Catherine Street West
Montreal, Quebec
CANADA H3H 1M7
www.interdec.qc.ca
Main #: (514) 939-4444
Fax #: (514) 939-3046

Kansas City Art Institute
4415 Warwick Boulevard
Kansas City, MO 64111
www.stamats.com/colleges/Pages/gallery8l.html
Main #: (816) 561-4852

Massachusetts Institute of Technology
77 Massachusetts Ave.
Cambridge, MA 02139
web.mit.edu
Undergrad. Admissions: (617) 253-2917
Computer Science: (617) 253-4600
Career Services: (617) 253-4733

National Animation and Design Centre
335 De Maisonneuve Blvd. E, #300
Montreal, Quebec
CANADA H2X 1K1
www.nad.qc.ca
Main #: (514) 288-3447
Fax #: (514) 288-5799

Ohio State University
1800 Cannon Dr.
Columbus, OH 43210
www.ohio-state.edu
Undergrad. Admissions: (614) 292-3980
Computer Science: (614) 292-5813
Career Services: (614) 292-6651

Pratt Institute
200 Willoughby Ave.
Brooklyn, NY 11205
www.pratt.edu
Main #: (800) 331-0834
Undergrad. Admissions: (718) 636-3600
Computer Graphics & Interactive Media: (718) 636-3411
Career Services: (718) 636-3506

Ringling School of Art and Design
2700 N. Tamiami Trail
Sarasota, FL 34234
www.vision.rsad.edu
Main #: (941) 351-5100
Undergrad. Admissions: (941) 359-7523
Center for Career Services: (941) 359-7501
Film/Video: (941) 359-7574

Rhode Island School of Design
Two College St.
Providence, RI 02903-2791
www.risd.edu
Main #: (401) 454-6100
Film/Video/Computer Animation: (401) 454-6233
Career Services: (401) 454-6620

Rochester Institute of Technology
One Lomb Memorial Dr.
Rochester, NY 14623-5608
www.rit.edu
Main #: (716)475-2411

San Francisco State University
1600 Holloway Ave.
San Francisco, CA 94132
www.sfsu.edu
3D Animation and Multimedia: (415) 338-1629
Multimedia/Film: (415) 338-1629
Career Services: (415) 338-1761
Multimedia Certificate Program: (415) 904-7700
Inter Arts: (415) 338-1478

Savannah College of Art and Design
548 E. Broughton St.
Savannah, GA 31401
www.scad.inter.net
Main #: (912) 238-2400
Computer Animation: (912) 238-2425
Director of Career Services: (912) 238-2401

School of Communication Arts
3220 Spring Forest Rd.
Raleigh, NC 27616
www.ncsca.com
Main #: 800-288-7442
Executive Director: Deborah Hooper
Director of Admissions: Wayne Moseley

School of Visual Arts
209 East. 23rd St.
New York, NY 10010
www.sva.edu
Undergrad. Admissions: (212) 592-2000
Film/Video/Animation: (212) 592-2180
Career Planning & Placement Ctr.: (212) 592-2373

Seneca College Digital Media Center
21 Beverly Hills Drive
Toronto, ON
CANADA M3L 1A2
dmc.senecac.on.ca
Main #: (416) 491-5050
Fax #: (416) 235-0462

Sheridan College
Schools of Communication Design
1430 Trafalgar Rd.
Oakville, ON
CANADA L6H 2L1
www.sheridanc.on.ca/wwwtst
Undergrad. Admissions: (905) 845-9430
Career Services: (905) 815-4046
Animation: (905) 845-9430 ext. 2579

Stanford University
Undergraduate Admissions
Old Union Bldg. 232
Stanford, CA 94305-3005
www-graphics.stanford.edu
Computer Graphics: (415) 725-3724
Career Services: (415) 723-3963

Texas A&M University
Visualization Program
A216 Langford Center
College Station, TX 77843-3137
www.tamu.edu
Main #: (409) 845-3211
TAMU Visualization Lab: (409) 845-3465
Career Services: (409) 845-5139

UCLA
Film and Television Dept.
405 Hilgard Ave.
Los Angeles, CA 90095
www.animation.filmtv.ucla.edu
Main #: (310) 825-4321
Animation Workshop: (310) 825-5829

University of British Columbia
2075 Wesbrook
Vancouver, BC
CANADA V6T 1Z2
www.ubc.ca
Main #: (604) 822-2211
Computer Science: (604) 822-3061
Career Services: (604) 822-4011

University of California at Berkeley
Undergraduate Admissions Office
110 Sproul Hall
Berkeley, CA 94720-5800
www.berkeley.edu
Undergrad. Admissions: (510) 642-3175
Dept. of Computer Science: (510) 642-3068
Career Planning/Placement: (510) 642-0464

University of North Carolina
College of Arts and Science
317 Steele Bldg. 3105
Chapel Hill, NC 27599-2200
www.unc.edu
Undergrad. Admissions: (919) 966-3621
Computer Science: (919) 962-1700
Career Services: (919) 962-6507

University of Southern California
School of CNTV
University Park
Los Angeles, CA 90089-2211
www.usc.edu
Main #: (213) 740-2311
Computer Animation: (213) 740-3985
Film: (213) 740-7679
Career Services: (213) 740-5627

University of Toronto
10 Kings College Rd.
Toronto, ON
CANADA M5S 364
www.utoronto.ca
Main #: (416) 978-2011
Computer Graphics: (416) 978-6025
Career Services: (416) 978-8000

University of Utah
Department of Admissions
201 South 1480 East Room 2505
Salt Lake City, UT 84112-9057
www.utah.edu
Main #: (801) 581-7281
Computer Graphics: (801) 585-4357
Career Services: (801) 581-6186

University of Washington
Box 355840
Seattle, WA 98195
www.washington.edu
Main #: (206) 543-2100
Undergrad. Admissions: (206) 543-9686
Computer Science: (206) 543-1695
Career Services: (206) 543-0535

VanArts
837 Beatty Street, 2nd Floor
Vancouver, BC
CANADA V6B 2M6
www.vanarts.bc.ca
Main #: (800) 396-2787
Fax #: (604) 684-2789

Vancouver Film School
1168 Hamilton St. #400
Vancouver, BC
CANADA V6B 2S2
www.multimedia.edu
Main #: (604) 685-6331

Appendix B:
Animation & Digital Effects Studios

The following is a selected list of studios producing interactive media, commercials, visual effects, and character animation for television and feature films. Explore the websites of each studio to find information on past projects, job opportunities, and submission guidelines.

3DO Company
600 Galveston Dr.
Redwood City, CA 94063
www.3do.com
Main #: (650) 261-3000
Fax #: (650) 261-3120

4-Front Design
1500 Broadway, Suite 509
New York, NY 10036
www.4-frontdesign.com

525 Post Production
6424 Santa Monica Blvd.
Hollywood, CA 90038
www.525post.com
Main #: (213) 525-1234
Fax #: (213) 467-3920

Activision Inc.
3100 Ocean Park Blvd.
Santa Monica, CA 90405
www.activision.com
Main #: (310) 255-2000
Fax #: (310) 255-2166

Algorithm Inc.
Atlanta, GA
www.algorithm.com
Main #: (770) 232-4949
Fax #: (770) 232-4951

Angel Studios
5966 La Place Court, Suite 170
Carlsbad, CA 92008
www.angel.com
Main #: (760) 929-0700
Fax #: (760) 929-0719

Available Light Ltd.
1152 S. Flower Street
Burbank, CA 91502
www.availablelightltd.com
Main #: (818) 842-2109

Banned From the Ranch Entertainment
2048 Broadway
Santa Monica, CA 90404
Main #: (310) 1313
Fax #: (310) 449-1315

Bethesda Softworks
(a Division of Media Technology
Ltd.)
1370 Piccard Drive, Suite 120
Rockville, MD 20850
www.bethsoft.com
Main #: (301) 926-8300
Fax #: (301) 926-8010

Big Idea Productions
168 N. Clinton, 6th Floor
Chicago, IL 60661
www.bigidea.com
Main #: (312) 669-1400

The Big Machine
51 Derry Street
Merrimack, NH 03054
www.bigmachine.com

Blizzard Entertainment
Blizzard North
654 Bair Island Road, #200
Redwood City, CA 94063
www.blizzard.com

Blue Sky Studios
One South Road
Harrison, NY 10528
www.blueskystudios.com
Main #: (914) 381-8400
Fax #: (914) 381-9791

Blur Studio
1130 Abbot Kinney Blvd.
Venice, CA 90291
www.blur.com
Main #: (310) 581-8848
Fax #: (310) 581-8850

Buzz F/X
312 Sherbrooke Street East
Montreal, Quebec
Canada H2X 1E6
www.buzzimage.com

The Chandler Group
4121 Redwood Ave.
Los Angels, CA 90066
Main #: (310) 305-7431
Fax #: (310) 306-2532

Cinar Animation
1055 Rene-Levesque Blvd. East
Montreal, Quebec
Canada H2L 4S5
www.cinar.com
Main #: (514) 843-8889
Fax #: (514) 843-7488

Cinesite Digital Studios
1017 N. Las Palmas, Suite 300
Hollywood, CA 90038
www.cinesite.com
Main #: (213) 468-4459
Fax #: (213) 468-5799

Computer Cafe, Inc.
3130 Skyway Drive, Suite 603
Santa Maria, CA 93455
www.computercafe.com
Main #: (805) 922-9479
Fax #: (805) 922-3225

**Computer Film Co.,
Los Angeles**
8522 National Blvd., Suite 103
Culver City, CA 90232
www.cfcla.com
Main #: (310) 838-3456
Fax #: (310) 838-1713

C.O.R.E. Digital Pictures
157 Princess Street, Suite 300
Toronto, ON
Canada M5A 4M4
www.coredp.com
Main #: (416) 367-2673
Fax #: (416) 367-4373

Crawford Digital
544 Armour Circle
Atlanta, GA 30324
Main #: (800) 831-8027

Crystal Dynamics
64 Willow Place
Menlo Park, CA 94025
www.crystald.com
Main #: (415) 473-3397
Fax #: (415) 473-3410

Curious Pictures Corporation
440 Lafayette, 6th Floor
New York, NY 10003
www.curiouspictures.com
Main #: (212) 674-1400
Fax #: (212) 674-0081

1360 Mission Street, Suite 201
San Francisco, CA 94103
Main #: (415) 437-1400
Fax #: (415) 437-1408

Digiscope
(Digital Visual Effects)
2308 Broadway
Santa Monica, CA 90404
www.digiscope.com
Main #: (310) 315-6060
Fax #: (310) 828-5856

Digital Anvil
316 Congress Avenue
Austin, TX 78701
www.digitalanvil.com
Main #: (512) 457-0129
Fax #: (512) 457-0403

Digital Artworks
40 E. Broadway, Suite 120
Eugene, OR 97401
www.digitalartworks.com
Main #: (541) 344-6541
Fax #: (541) 683-3576

Digital Domain
300 Rose Avenue
Venice, CA 90291
www.d2.com
Main #: (310) 314-2934
Fax #: (310) 314-2888
Jobline #: (310) 314-2934

Digital Muse
1337 Third Street Promenade,
3rd Floor
Santa Monica, CA 90401
www.dmuse.com
Main #: (310) 656-8050
Fax #: (310) 656-8055

Dimensional Studios
351 Ninth Street, 3rd Floor
San Francisco, CA 94103
www.dstudios.com
Main #: (415) 241-9900
Fax #: (415) 241-9980

Disney-MGM Studios
P.O. Box 10200
Film-TV Dept.
Bungalow 2
Lake Buena Vista, FL 32830
Main #: (407) 560-5736
Fax #: (407) 560-2830

Walt Disney Imagineering
1401 Flower Street
Glendale, CA 91221
Main #: (818) 544-6500

**Walt Disney
Feature Animation**
500 S. Buena Vista Street
Burbank, CA 91521
Main #: (818) 526-3042
Fax #: (818) 558-2575

Walt Disney Studios
500 S. Buena Vista Street
Burbank, CA 91521
Main #: (818) 560-1000

**Walt Disney
Buena Vista
Post Production Services**
500 S. Buena Vista Street
Burbank, CA 91521
Main #: (818) 560-5513

DKP Effects
1321 7th Street, Suite 300
Santa Monica, CA 90401
www.dkp.com
Main #: (310) 458-0678
Fax #: (310) 458-7759

Dream Quest Images
2365 Park Center Drive
Simi Valley, CA 93065
www.dqimages.com
Main #: (805) 578-3100
Fax #: (805) 583-4673

Dream Theater
16134 Hart Street
Van Nuys, CA 91404
www.dreamtheater.com
Main #: (818) 376-8480
Fax #: (818) 376-8484

Dreamworks SKG
1000 Flower Street
Glendale, CA 90201
www.dreamworksanim.com
Main #: (818) 695-7252

**Duck Soup
Produckions, Inc.**
2205 Stoner Avenue
Los Angeles, CA 90064
www.ducksoupla.com
Main #: (310) 478-0771
Fax #: (310) 478-0773

Encore Hollywood
6344 Fountain Avenue
Hollywood, CA 90028
www.encorevideo.com
Main #: (323) 466-7663
Fax #: (323) 467-5539

Encore Santa Monica
6702 Arizona Avenue
Santa Monica, CA 90401
www.encorevideo.com
Main #: (310) 656-7663
Fax #: (310) 656-7699

Flamdoodle Animation, Inc.
6 Cuesta Lane
Santa Fe, NM 87505
www.flamdoodle.com
Main #: (505) 982-3132
Fax #: (505) 466-3525

Flying Foto Factory, Inc.
P.O. Box 1166
Durham, NC 27702
www.flyingfoto.com
Main #: (919) 682-3411
Fax #: (919) 688-7886

Foundation Imaging
27525 Newhall Ranch Road, #9
Valencia, CA 91355
www.foundation-i.com
Main #: (805) 257-0292
Fax #: (805) 257-7966

Framestore
9 Noel Street
London
ENGLAND W1V 4AL
www.framestore.co.uk
Main #: +44 (0) 171-208-2600
Fax #: +44 (0) 171-208-2626

Future-Primitive
2054 San Jose Avenue
Alameda, CA 94501
www.future-primitive.com
Main #: (510) 769-1034

Gadjecki Visual Effects
29 Booth Avenue, Suite 205
Toronto, ON
Canada M4M 2M3
Main #: (416) 463-6753
Fax #: (416) 463-7312

Gear Productions
6404 Hollywood Blvd., Suite 424
Hollywood, CA 90028
www.gearprod.com
Main #: (323) 466-4327
Fax #: (323) 466-0546

GT Interactive
175 West 200 South, Suite 1000
Salt Lake City, UT 84101
www.gtinteractive.com
Fax #: (801) 994-5180

Home Run Pictures
100 First Avenue, #450
Pittsburgh, PA 15222
www.hrpictures.com
Main #: (412) 391-8200
Fax #: (412) 391-1772

hOuse of mOves
Motion Capture Studios
711 Hampton Drive
Venice, CA 90291
www.moves.com
Main #: (310) 399-2485
Fax #: (310) 399-9115

Ikonic
2 Harrison Street
San Francisco, CA 94105
www.ikonic.com
Main #: (415) 908-8000
Fax #: (415) 908-8100

51 E. 42nd Street, Suite 400
New York, NY 10017
Main #: (212) 681-9090
Fax #: (212) 681-9096

JAM Studios
P.O. Box 15006
Rio Rancho, NM 87174
www.jamstudios.com
Fax #: (505) 896-6812

Janimation
840 Exposition
Dallas, TX 75226
www.janimation.com
Main #: (214) 823-7760

Kleiser-Walczak
Construction Co.
87 Marshall Street, Bldg. 1
Northadams, MA 01247
www.kwcc.com
Main #: (413) 664-7441
Fax #: (413) 664-7442

6315 Yucca Street
Hollywood, CA 90028

Konami Computer
Entertainment
900 Deerfield Parkway
Buffalo Grove, IL 60098
www.konami.com
Main #: (847) 215-5100
Fax #: (847) 215-5137

Lamb & Company
2429 Nicollet Avenue South
Minneapolis, MN 55404
www.lamb.com
Main #: (612) 872-1000
Fax #: (612) 879-5776

Live Wire
Productions & VFX
28631 S. Western Avenue, Ste. 101
Ranchos Palos Verdes, CA 90275
Main #: (310) 831-6227
Fax #: (310) 547-3456

L-Squared Entertainment
530 Wilshire Blvd., Suite 401
Santa Monica, CA 90401
www.lsqr.com
Main #: (310) 587-2100
Fax #: (310) 587-2121

Lucasart Entertainment
Company
P.O. Box 10307
San Rafael, CA 94912
www.lucasarts.com
Fax #: (415) 444-8438

Lucas Learning Ltd.
P.O. Box 10667
San Rafael, CA 94912
www.lucasarts.com
Main # (415) 444-8800
Fax #: (415) 444-8898
Jobline #: (415) 444-8899

Lucas Digital Ltd.
Industrial
Light & Magic (ILM)
Skywalker Sound
P.O. Box 2459
San Rafael, CA 94912
www.ldlhr.com
www.ilm-jobs.com
Jobline #: (415) 258-2100

Lumeni Productions, Inc.
1632 Flower Street
Glendale, CA 91201
Main #: (818) 956-2200
Fax #: (818) 956-3298

**Mainframe
Entertainment Inc.**
1045 Howe Street, Suite 710
Vancouver, BC
Canada V6Z 2A9
www.mainframe.bc.ca
Main #: (604) 681-3595
Fax #: (604) 681-3517

Manex Studios
1040 W. Midway
Alameda, CA 94501
www.manex-group.com
Main #: (510) 864-0600
Fax #: (510) 864-9669

Matte World Digital
24 Digital Drive, #6
Novato, CA 94949
www.matteworld.com
Main #: (415) 382-1929

Metrolight Studios
5724 W. Third Street, Suite 400
Los Angeles, CA 90036
www.metrolight.com
Main #: (213) 932-0400
Fax #: (213) 932-8440

Mondo Media
135 Mississippi Street, 3rd Floor
San Francisco, CA 94107
www.mondomed.com
Main #: (415) 865-2700
Fax #: (415) 865-2645

Mozes Cleveland & Company
183 E. Boston Mills Road
Hudson, OH 44264
www.mozescleveland.com
Main #: (330) 528-0029
Fax #: (330) 528-3445

Neoscape, Inc.
700 Massachusetts Avenue,
2nd Floor
Cambridge, MA 02139
www.neoscape.com
Main #: (617) 354-1085
Fax #: (617) 354-1065

**Nickelodeon
Animation Studios**
231 W. Olive
Burbank, CA 91502
www.nick.com
Main #: (818) 736-3039
Fax #: (818) 736-3539

Origin Systems
5918 W. Courtyard Drive
Austin, TX 78730
www.origin.ea.com
Main #: (512) 434-4357
Fax #: (512) 346-7905

Pacific Data Images (PDI)
3101 Park Blvd.
Palo Alto, CA 94306
www.pdi.com
Main #: (650) 846-8100
Fax #: (650) 846-8101

Pacific Title Mirage Studio Digital Division
1149 N. Gower Street
Hollywood, CA 90038
www.pactitle.com
Main #: (323) 769-3700
Fax #: (323) 769-3701

Pinnacle Studios
2334 Elliot Avenue
Seattle, WA 98121
www.pinnaclestudios.com
Main #: (206) 441-9878
Fax #: (206) 728-2266

Pixar Animation Studios
1001 W. Cutting Blvd.
Richmond, CA 94804
www.pixar.com
Main #: (800) 888-9856
Fax #: (510) 236-0388
Jobline #: (510) 236-4000

Pix n Stones Production
326 Sanchez Street
San Francisco, CA 94114
www.pixnstones.com
Main #: (415) 558-9332
Fax #: (415) 626-7680

Planet Three Animation Studio
1223 N. 23rd Street
Wilmington, NC 28405
www.planet3animation.com
Main #: (910) 343-3720
Fax #: (910) 343-3722

Planet 9 Studios
2 Harrison Street, #145
San Francisco, CA 94105
www.planet9.com
Main #: (415) 247-7997
Fax #: (415) 543-7037

Platinum Pictures Multimedia Inc.
3627 Pine Knoll Drive South
Baraboo, WI 53913
www.platinumpictures.com
Main #: (608) 355-1097
Fax #: (608) 355-0499

P.O.P. Animation (Pacific Ocean Post)
1546 7th Street, Suite 200
Santa Monica, CA 90401
www.popstudios.com
Main #: (310) 393-4699
Fax #: (310) 393-4799

Post Group
6335 Homewood Avenue
Hollywood, CA 90028
www.postgroup.com
Main #: (323) 462-2300
Fax #: (323) 462-0386

Pyros Pictures
1201 Dove Street, Suite 550
Newport Beach, CA 92660
www.pyrospictures.com
Main #: (714) 833-0334
Fax #: (714) 833-8655

Rainbow Studios
3830 N. 7th Street
Phoenix, AZ 85014
www.rainbo.com
Fax #: (602) 230-2553

Reality Bytes Inc.
One Kendall Square, Bldg. 400
Cambridge, MA 02139
www.realbytes.com
Main #: (617) 621-2500
Fax #: (617) 621-2581

Reality Check Studios
723 North Cahuenga Bvd.
Hollywood, CA 90038
www.realityx.com
Main #: (323) 465-3900

Red Storm Entertainment
2000 Aerial Center, SDuite 110
Morrisville, NC 27560
www.redstorm.com
Main #: (919) 460-1776
Fax #: (919) 468-3305

Rezn8 Productions
6430 Sunset Blvd., Suite 100
Hollywood, CA 90028
www.rezn8.com
Main #: (213) 957-2162

R/Greenberg Associates
R/GA Interactive
350 W. 39th Street
New York, NY 10018
www.rga.com
Main #: (212) 946-4000
Fax #: (212) 946-4010

Rhythm & Hues Studios
5404 Jandy Place
Los Angeles, CA 90066
www.rhythm.com
Main #: (310) 448-7500
Fax #: (310) 448-7600

Sierra On-Line
3380 146th Place SE, Suite 300
Bellevue, WA 98007
www.sierra.com
Main #: (425) 649-9800
Fax #: (425) 641-7617

Sony Pictures Imageworks
9050 W. Washington Blvd.
Culver City, CA 90232
www.spiw.com
Main #: (310) 840-8000
Fax #: (310) 840-8888

Special Designs Studios
P.O. Box 1916
Studio City, CA 91614
www.sdas.com
Main #: (818) 766-9766
Fax #: (818) 766-9716

Square USA Inc.
4640 Admiralty Way, Suite 1200
Marina del Rey, CA 90292
www.sqla.com
Fax #: (310) 302-9550

55 Merchant Street, Suite 3100
Honolulu, HI 96813
Fax #: (808) 535-9100

Stargate Films, Inc.
1103 W. Isabel Street
Burbank, CA 91506
www.stargatefilms.com
Main #: (818) 972-1100
Fax #: (818) 972-9411

Station X Studios
1717 Stewart Street
Santa Monica, CA 90404
www.stationxstudios.com
Main #: (310) 828-6460
Fax #: (310) 828-4101

Stormfront Studios Inc.
4040 Civic Center Drive
San Rafael, CA 94903
www.stormfrontstudios.com
Main #: (415) 479-2800
Fax #: (415) 479-2880

**Tiburon
Entertainment, Inc.**
P.O. Box 940427
Maitland, FL 32794
www.tibent.com

Tippett Studio
2741 10th Street
Berkeley, CA 94710
Main #: (510) 649-9711
Fax #: (510) 649-9399

Title House / THDX
738 N. Cahuenga Blvd.
Hollywood, CA 90038
www.titlehouse.com
Main #: (323) 469-1611
Fax #: (323) 469-0377

TOPIX/Mad Dog
35 McCaul Street, Suite 200
Toronto, ON
Canada M5T 1V7
www.topix.com
Main #: (416) 971-7711
Fax #: (416) 971-9277

Viewpoint Digital
625 South State Street
Orem, UT 84058
www.viewpoint.com
Fax #: (801) 229-3302

**Vision Art
Design and Animation**
3025 Olympic Blvd.
Santa Monica, CA 90404
www.visionart.com
Main #: (310) 264-5566
Fax #: (310) 264-5572

**Warner Brothers
Classic Animation
Warner Brothers
Television Animation**
15303 Ventura Blvd., #1200
Sherman Oaks, CA 91403
www.wbsf.com
Main #: (818) 977-8534
Fax #: (818) 977-8152

Waterland Productions
17351 Murphy Avenue
Irvine, CA 92614
www.waterlandfilms.com
Main #: (949) 582-7631
Fax #: (949) 582-7642

Will Vinton Studios
1400 NW 22nd Avenue
Portland, OR 97210
www.vinton.com
Main #: (503) 225-1130
Fax #: (503) 226-3746

WunderFilm Design
7700 W. Sunset Blvd., Suite 200
Los Angeles, CA 90046
www.wunderfilm.com
Main #: (323) 845-4100
Fax #: (323) 845-4101

XL Translab
(a Division of Media Technology
Ltd.)
1370 Piccard Drive, Suite 120
Rockville, MD 20850
www.xltranslab.com
Main #: (301) 926-8300
Fax #: (301) 948-2253

Appendix C:
Additional Resources

The following is a selected list of additional resources (many mentioned throughout this book) which you'll find useful as your skills develop.

Magazines, Books & Directories

3D Artist Magazine
P.O. Box 4787
Santa Fe, NM 87502
www.3dartist.com
Main #: (505) 424-8945
Fax #: (505) 424-8946

3D Design Magazine
525 Market Street, Suite 500
San Francisco, CA 94105
www.3d-design.com
Main #: (800) 234-4286
Fax #: (615) 377-0525

***Animals in Motion**, and
The Human Figure in Motion*
by Eadweard Muybridge
Dover Publications, Inc.
31 East 2nd Street
Mineola, NY 11501

Animation Magazine
30101 Agoura Court, Suite 110
Agoura Hills, CA 91301-4301
www.animag.com
Main #: (818) 991-2884
Fax #: (818) 991-3773

Blu-Book
(Film, TV & Commercial
Production Directory)
The Hollywood Reporter
5055 Wilshire Blvd., 6th Floor
Los Angeles, CA 90036
Main #: (323) 525-2000
Order #: (323) 525-2150

Cinefex
P.O. Box 20027
Riverside, CA 92516
www.cinefex.com
Main #: (909) 781-1917
Fax #: (909) 788-1793

Computer Graphics World
98 Spit Brook Road, 1st Floor
Nashua, NH 03062-5737
www.cgw.com
Main #: (603) 891-0123
Fax #: (603) 891-0539

***Disney Animation:
The Illusion of Life***
by Frank Thomas
& Ollie Johnston
Hyperion Press
114 Fifth Avenue
New York, NY 10011

Film & Video Magazine
8455 Beverly Blvd., Suite 508
Los Angeles, CA 90048
Main #: (323) 653-8053
Fax #: (323) 653-8190

**Handbook Pricing
& Ethical Guidelines**
Graphic Artists Guild
90 John Street, Suite 403
New York, NY 10038-3202
www.gag.org
Main #: (212) 791-3400
Fax #: (212) 791-0333

Post Magazine
270 Madison Avenue, 5th Floor
New York, NY 10016-0685
www.postmagazine.com
Main #: (212) 951-6600
Fax #: (212) 951-6717

Software
& Hardware

3D Studio Max
Kinetix, a division of Autodesk
642 Harrison Street
San Francisco, CA 94107
www.ktx.com
Main #: (415) 547-2000
Fax #: (415) 547-2222

Animation Master
Hash Inc.
2800 East Evergreen Blvd.
Vancouver, WA 98661
www.hash.com
Main #: (360) 750-0042
Fax #: (360) 750-0451

Houdini
Side Effects Software
477 Richmond St.West, Suite 1001
Toronto, ON
CANADA M5V 3E7
www.sidefx.com
Main #: (416) 504-9876
Fax #: (416) 504-6648

233 Wilshire Blvd., Suite 610
Santa Monica, CA 90401
Main #: (310) 319-9876
Fax #: (310) 319-6264

LightWave 3D, Inspire
Newtek, Inc.
Fountainhead One
8200 IH-10 West, Suite 900
San Antonio, TX 78230
www.newtek.com
Main #: (800) 843-8934
Fax #: (800) 854-7111

Maya
Alias/Wavefront
(a subsidiary of
Silicon Graphics, Inc.)
210 King Street East
Toronto, ON
CANADA M5A 1J7
www.aw.sgi.com
Main #: (416) 362-9181
Fax #: (416) 369-6140

Perception Video Recorder
Digital Processing Systems, Inc.
11 Spiral Drive, Suite 10
Florence, Ky 41042
www.dps.com
Main #: (800) 775-3314
Fax #: (606) 371-3729

Ray Dream 3D
Ray Dream Studio
Metacreations
6303 Carpinteria
Carpinteria, CA 93013
www.metacreations.com
Main #: (714) 557-1636
Fax #: (714) 434-7652

Renderman Products
Pixar
1001 W. Cutting Blvd.
Richmond, CA 94804
www.pixar.com/products/
renderman/renderman.html
Main #: (800) 888-9856
Fax #: (510) 236-0388

Softimage
Softimage-Headquarters
3510 St-Laurent Blvd
Montreal, QC
CANADA H2X 2V2
www.softimage.com
Main #: (514) 845-1636
Fax #: (514) 845-5676

Organizations

Animation World Network
World Headquarters
6525 Sunset Blvd.
Garden Suite 10
Hollywood, CA 90028
www.awn.com
Main #: (323) 468-2554
Fax #: (323) 464-5914

Association of Computing
Machinery (ACM)
Headquarters Office
One Astor Plaza
1515 Broadway
New York, NY 10036 USA
info.acm.org
Main #: +1-212-869-7440
Fax Numbers:
Membership/General:
    +1-212-944-1318
SIG Services: +1-212-302-5826
Publications: +1-212-869-0481

SIGGRAPH
ACM's Special Interest Group
on Computer Graphics
www.siggraph.org

Graphic Artists Guild
90 John Street, Suite 403
New York, NY 10038-3202
www.gag.org
Main #: (212) 791-3400
Fax #: (212) 791-0333

IATSE
Motion Picture Screen
Cartoonists and Affiliated
Optical Electronic and
Graphics Arts, Local 839
4729 Lankershim Boulevard,
North Hollywood, CA 91602-1864
www.primenet.com/~mpsc839
Main #: (818) 766-7151
Fax #: (818) 506-4805

Index

ORDER FORM

COMPUTER ANIMATION
EXPERT ADVICE ON BREAKING INTO THE BUSINESS

by DALE K. MYERS

A street-smart guide on how to break into the field of computer animation and digital visual effects, including candid tips from animators, producers, and directors working at today's top animation studios.

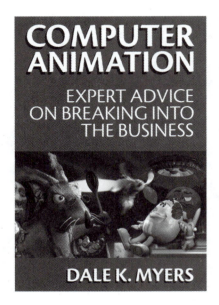

$19.95 (U.S. funds Postpaid)
ISBN: 0-9662709-6-7
6x9 in. Softcover 160 pp.

Oak Cliff Press, Inc., P.O. Box 608-C, Milford, MI 48381-0608, Tele: (248)676-8084 / Fax: (248)684-9038

Yes! Please send ____ copies of *Computer Animation: Expert Advice on Breaking into the Business*, by Dale K. Myers, at $19.95 each (U.S. funds/Postpaid)(MI residents add $1.20 sales tax) to:

Name: _____

Organization: _____

Street Address: _____ Suite/Apt: _____

City: _____ State: _____ Postal Code: _____

Province/Country: _____

Visa/Mastercard/Discover/Amex(circle one): _____ Exp: _____

(If different than above) Credit Card Billing Address Number: _____ Postal Code: _____

Makes checks payable to: Oak Cliff Press, Inc., and mail to: Oak Cliff Press, Inc., P.O. Box 608-C, Milford, MI 48381-0608. All orders ship First Class within 48 hours of receipt. Allow 3-10 days for delivery.
Order on-line at: www.oakcliffpress.com / email: dmyers@oakcliffpress.com